COWBOY UP!

Alan Day has put together a delightful collection of vignettes ranging from his childhood days on the Lazy B Ranch to his time running the wild mustang ranch in South Dakota. I found myself chuckling one minute and crying the next as he reflected on an assortment of adventures and the characters he met along the way.

—**Jan Cleere**, author of *Never Don't Pay Attention: The Life of Rodeo Photographer Louise L. Serpa, Levi's & Lace: Arizona Women Who Made History, Outlaw Tales of Arizona,* and *More than Petticoats*

Alan Day has given us a lively collection of life lessons learned working and living on the Lazy B. With the eagle eyes of Lynn Wiese Sneyd, each story is a well-written fable employing horses, sometimes cows, dogs and other critters, and even an airplane. Grouped into seven categories, each one introduced by an epigram of cowboy wisdom like, "Life is simpler when you plow around the stump," this collection is enjoyable and fun to read.

—**Richard Collins**, C6 Ranch, author of *Riding Behind the Padre*

There is nothing more American than cowboys. Alan Day is a real American cowboy and has the stories to prove it. We're all better off for getting to know Alan and the western way of life.

—**Russell True**, owner of White Stallion Dude Ranch and author of *Dude Ranching in Arizona*

COWBOY UP!
LIFE LESSONS
from
LAZY B

H. ALAN DAY
with LYNN WIESE SNEYD

NEW YORK

NASHVILLE • MELBOURNE • VANCOUVER

COWBOY UP!
LIFE LESSONS *from* LAZY B

Published in New York, New York, by Morgan James Publishing. Morgan James is a trademark of Morgan James, LLC. www.MorganJamesPublishing.com

The Morgan James Speakers Group can bring authors to your live event. For more information or to book an event visit The Morgan James Speakers Group at www.TheMorganJamesSpeakersGroup.com.

ISBN 978-1-68350-398-9 paperback
ISBN 978-1-68350-399-6 eBook
Library of Congress Control Number: 2017900289

Cover Design by:
Rachel Lopez
www.r2cdesign.com

Interior Design by:
Bonnie Bushman
The Whole Caboodle Graphic Design

In an effort to support local communities, raise awareness and funds, Morgan James Publishing donates a percentage of all book sales for the life of each book to Habitat for Humanity Peninsula and Greater Williamsburg.

Get involved today! Visit
www.MorganJamesBuilds.com

For Sandra and Ann

TABLE OF CONTENTS

Part 3: ON COMMON SENSE 65

Never kick a cow chip on a hot day.

Part 4: ON LISTENING 93

Never miss a good chance to shut up.

Part 5: ON PERSISTENCE 123

If Plan A doesn't work, stay calm. The alphabet has twenty-five more letters.

ACKNOWLEDGEMENTS

Just as it takes more than one cowboy to wrangle a herd of cattle, it takes more than one writer to wrangle a book. Special thanks go to Terry Whalin and the talented, professional team at Morgan James. Another shout out to editors Margo Barnes, Nancy Wiese, and Lauren Hagan, as well as readers Diana Madaras, Rod Miller, and Richard Collins. Creative suggestions were offered by all. If it weren't so corny, we'd say this book was an exercise in team penning. Well, we'll say it anyway. Our team got the steer in the pen and a book on the shelf, and it doesn't get much better than that.

INTRODUCTION

I'm a third generation Arizonan. Back in 1880, my granddad settled the Lazy B ranch in the Duncan Valley of what would later become eastern Arizona. At the time, Geronimo was running around getting his kicks terrorizing the locals. Family lore has it that Granddad had a brush up with Geronimo while moving some horses from Animus, New Mexico to our ranch headquarters. While camped out overnight, he heard Indians start rustling his horses. He didn't want to confront them because he wanted to live another day, so he hunkered down in his bedroll. The Indians took all the horses and left him his life. When Granddad died, my dad took over managing Lazy B. Under his guidance, it became a 200,000-acre, high desert ranch straddling the Arizona and New Mexico territories. When my dad retired, I took over managing the ranch. Lazy B is so much a part of me that I swear its soil still runs through my blood.

Growing up, I probably had the greatest young life of anybody I know. I had a huge playground and it was all mine, meaning that I had access to every inch of the ranch. I was never bored. An adventure awaited me around every bend. Back then, the deal was if you thought you were big enough to do something, and I don't care if it was swim across the river or ride a horse or climb a windmill, if you thought you were big enough, then just help yourself. Go ahead and do it. And if you weren't big enough, you'd fail and learn something in the process. The only ranch rule: Be home by supper.

By the time I came along, my parents—I won't say they didn't care—they just didn't pay a lot of attention to what I was doing. I was the youngest of three kids. DA and MO, which was what my sisters and I called my parents, were spending their energy getting my oldest sister Sandra through Stanford University and launching her career. As they should have been. Sandra was ten years older than I and was a superstar from day one. I tell people I have the best job in the world and that's being Sandra Day O'Connor's brother. She's one of the sweetest, kindest, and biggest people you could ever meet, and always has been someone you could look up to and be inspired by. Well, I came along and didn't quite have those superstar qualities. Don't get me wrong. I'm not complaining one bit. Some kids would feel left out, but I felt that the world was my oyster, and I could do whatever I wanted. Talk about a wild child! I was that. Once in a while I'd go a little too far, but I'd get reined back pretty quick.

I attended the local high school in Duncan, Arizona, but managed to get kicked out during junior year. I graduated from high school in El Paso while living with my grandmother. My parents didn't come to my graduation, but then again they hadn't come to any of my football games in Duncan or other activities in any grade. After graduation, I went home to the ranch and went to work. I never really thought about doing anything else. I loved the ranch. I got about halfway through that summer after high school graduation when my mother got a hold of me one day.

"Have you thought about college?" she asked.

I said, "No, not really."

"Well, would you be interested in college?"

"I don't know. Never thought about it. Yeah. Okay. I guess so."

She wanted to know where I'd like to go.

"Well, I dunno," I said. "Hadn't even thought about it. Where should I go?"

"Would you consider the University of Arizona?" She had graduated from there in 1925, so she liked the idea.

"Okay," I said. "Sounds all right to me."

She said she'd get the papers and get me registered. And so she did.

About the first of August, MO told me it was almost time to go to college, and I needed to go down to the store and buy some new Levis and a couple of shirts. So I went down to Duncan and bought some new clothes.

Pretty soon, she rounded me up and said, "It's time to go to college."

I looked at her. "Where is the University of Arizona?" I didn't know.

"It's in Tucson," she replied.

I had never been to Tucson. "Where's Tucson?"

She said, "Get in your car, go to Lordsburg, and turn right."

And that's how I went to college.

I was on campus for about ten minutes and decided it was the neatest place I had ever been. So many people and more pretty girls than I even knew existed in the world. My dad gave me two hundred dollars per month with the understanding that I never was to ask for more. I supplemented the windfall by scooping ice cream at Baskin Robbins, playing bridge and poker, and working on the ranch during breaks. I made the dean's list and was scheduled to graduate on time, but I was having so much fun, I applied to law school and was accepted. I sure as hell didn't want to be a lawyer; I'd always planned to go back to the ranch. I just wanted three more years at the University of Arizona.

Much to my surprise, my parents came to my college graduation. I had my degree for all of two minutes when my mother grabbed my arm and said, "Young man, your father's sick. The ranch is going to hell. Now get over there and go to work."

I said, " Yes ma' am. I'll be there tomorrow."

I managed Lazy B for the next forty years. With no upcoming generations interested in taking it over, I sold the ranch in 1994. During my years on Lazy B, I had more adventures than I ever could have imagined. You can't do something that long and in the big way that ranching requires without learning quite a little about life. So here I am to share those adventures, lessons, and wisdom with you. There are teachers, some two-footed, some four-legged, even some with feathers. There are adventures set on the ranch, a few in the city, and some in the air. There are mistakes, victories, and everything in between. No matter who you are, where you are, or what you do, at some point in life, you have to face what's in front of you, and the only way to do that is with a little bit of luck, lots of guts, and hopefully a handful of hard-earned wisdom. So take what appeals to you and pack it in your saddlebag. Maybe there'll be a spot along the trail where you can use it. Maybe not. Either way, enjoy the ride.

PART 1

ON FRIENDSHIP

When you're in jail, a good friend will be trying to bail you out. A best friend will be in the next cell saying, "Damn that was fun!"

CHAPTER 1

CHICO AND THE DOG

My first horse was a little mustang named Chico. A local cowboy captured him from a herd of wild horses on the flanks of Steeple Rock Mountain, just north of Lazy B. Somehow my dad ended up with him before I was born, so my sisters Sandra and Ann also claim him as their first horse.

Chico became my best friend almost as soon as I could walk. A pretty bay color with a star on his forehead, he was a small horse, too small for a cowboy, but just right for a child. The kid horse of all kid horses, he took care of me as much as my mother and probably just as well. When I grew big enough to saddle Chico and could open the corral gate, we could go ten miles in any direction and still be on Lazy B. Chico and I would have amazing adventures. One day I'd be out there riding Chico, and in my imagination, I'd be the world's best cowboy.

A wild bull would be out running loose, and I'd rope him, dally up, and drag him back to the herd. All the other cowboys would say, "Wow, what a cowboy he is!" Then the next day, I'd be the Indian who had escaped from the cavalry, and I'd be sneaking down the sand washes looking for soldiers.

Chico would go at a speed I was capable of handling and no faster. When he jumped a ditch or dodged a mesquite bush, I sometimes fell off. Whenever I fell, Chico would stop, even mid-stride, and not go one step forward until I climbed back on him. I'd usually get a pretty good thump on the ground and get up crying. I'd blame Chico for my fall. Of course, it was never his fault. But there I was, a small, angry, pouty kid. I'd go up and kick him in the shins to show him just how angry I was. He still didn't move. Then I'd get back in the saddle, and we'd continue with our adventure. I rode Chico the first time I was allowed to go on a roundup when I was five years old. He kept me safe, and more importantly, he helped me make a hand. He was my best friend, and I loved him.

Eventually the day came to retire Chico. He was nearing thirty, and it was time for him to enjoy a pension of fresh grass on a pretty pasture. Chico had made friends with our resident ranch dog, a boxer named Chap. I swear that dog loved Chico as much as I did. Chico would amble through the corral, Chap trotting right next to him. The two would head out to pasture together. This best-buddy relationship had to be tough on Chap because dogs need water every few hours, and Lazy B's desert pasture had no freestanding water. When the duo returned to headquarters, Chap plunged into the water trough, rolled around like an otter in a pond, and drank so much water that I thought it would spout from his ears. Since he wasn't a hunter, he filled up on food that we set out for him on the back porch. Chico patiently waited for a few hours while the refueling took place. Then, back out to the pasture the two went, coming and going as freely as they wanted.

One day, I saw Chap trotting past the corrals toward the barn, alone. Right then I knew Chico had passed. I quickly saddled up and whistled to Chap. We made our way to the pasture. As I suspected, we found Chico still as stone. The coyotes hadn't gotten to him yet. I knelt down and stroked his weathered hide, saw the peaceful look on his face. Chap nuzzled my shoulder. I knew Chico was old and it was his time, but still. You think you're prepared, but when someone you love dies, the loss comes as a shock.

My horse, my dog, and I walked back to headquarters, my face wet in the dry heat. Underneath the immediate grief glowed the permanent joy of having known Chico, of having him in my life for so long. Not only was he my first horse, he also was my first lesson in the meaning of loyalty, patience, and friendship. And even through tears and pain, how can you not be grateful for that?

To this day, I carry the memory of Chico. Sometimes I can't help but wonder if he were there in spirit during the four years I cared for the government's herd of wild horses on my ranch up in South Dakota. I like to think he was watching out for me. Maybe he even put in a good word with the herd and encouraged them to trust me. That would be Chico, calm as ever, steady and sure-footed, certain that things would work out. And somehow, they always did.

CHAPTER 2

PRICKLY PETS

Most cowboys are a sucker for a baby or crippled animal and will go completely out of their way to save a suffering youngster. Count me as one of those cowboys. One of the first rescues I made was during a Cub Scout overnight campout. My buddy Raymond Probert and I found two orphaned baby bobcats and decided it would be a good deed to bring them home. So he took one and I took one. I named mine Bobby.

My mother grudgingly welcomed Bobby into our home. He was a cute kitten and looked like the other cats milling around the back porch and barn except he had spikes of fur on the tips of his ears. I made a bed for him on the front porch. The other cats pretty much stuck to their territory and left him alone. When he settled in my lap, Bobby loved to be rubbed and purred like a house cat. I could pick him up, but if I made a quick reach for him, he'd take a chunk out of me. I soon had a handful of scars. We learned that he liked red meat, and my mother always made sure we had extra for Bobby.

Bobby and I played for hours. I'd hide in the backyard and call him. He'd come racing around to find me. Or not. Inside, where he spent quite a little time, he'd jump around on tables, on the mantle, on the piano. Susie, our terrier, knew not to squawk at him. If she had, he would have swatted her a good one. He was unpredictable enough that our cowboys and family friends didn't want to mess with him because they didn't know if they would get a purr or a bite. Still, I raised him to almost full-grown. He was a pretty golden color and had a short tail.

Raymond must have known more about bobcats because his turned out much more gentle, except for one habit. His cat would lay in wait for you behind a corner, then jump out, and scare the crap out of you. That cat had the shiniest, softest fur. Probably had something to do with Raymond feeding him cod liver oil. Raymond taught his cat to use the toilet. I figured Bobby was just more of an independent soul and was fine using the outdoors.

Bobby was less than a year old when I had to leave him at home during our summer family vacation. We piled in the car and left the ranch and Bobby in the care of the cowboys. A week later we returned. Bobby was nowhere to be seen.

"Where's Bobby?" I asked the cowboys as soon as I could.

They all shrugged. "When you left, he left," said one of them.

I felt bad about having left and worse that I wouldn't ever see Bobby again. It wasn't until years later one of the cowboys confessed that Vernon, a part-timer, hated Bobby and killed him the day after we drove out the ranch road. Well, that one stuck with me. I always aimed to do better than Vernon did, and I was given quite a few opportunities during my years on Lazy B.

One opportunity landed in my hands a few decades later. I had taken the jeep out to check on water levels in the holding tanks and to leave some fresh salt licks for the cows. While squatting on the ground next to one of the tanks, I heard a chorus of squeaks. Just inches in front of my boot, nestled in a clump of grass, were two baby javelinas, their eyes not yet open. Their pitiful cries indicated they were eager for mama to return with some milk. I followed a set of tracks and soon discovered why they were so hungry. Mama's carcass looked to be about a day old.

I scooped up one of the babies. It fit perfectly in my palm. The early summer morning still had a chill, so I grabbed a work glove from my back pocket and gently slid the baby inside it. Its twin went into the other glove. I settled the pair on the jeep floor and continued on my weekly round.

Back at headquarters, the first thing I did was wrangle up a bottle and nipple. We always kept them in stock to feed dogies and other orphans. Took me a bit to find one small enough for the tiny critters. I had one of the babies in my hand and was urging it to take the bottle when Cole Webb, the ranch foreman, came up.

"They're starving, but they won't eat," I said.

Cole frowned. "You'd think they'd like that warm milk."

We found a box and blanket, made a nest for the babies, and left them in the screened-in back porch of my house. We checked on them after lunch. Once again, those little rascals refused the nipple.

"I don't know if they'll make it another twenty-four hours," I said. Cole and I sat looking at the box. Neither of us wanted to give up on their lives.

"Well, maybe they don't like the nipple," Cole said. "Let's try a cup."

I had never seen an orphaned animal drink from a cup. I fetched a cup from the kitchen. Cole poured milk into it and held it to the baby's mouth. The baby started slurping. After a long drink, it turned its head, and for the first time all day, it stopped crying.

As soon as those babies knew where the milk was coming from, they adopted us as parents. Within weeks, they started following us everywhere around the ranch. They were funny little creatures with habits I never anticipated. If I sat down, I'd have one in my lap looking for attention and a warm hand. If I went in the house, I'd find them waiting for me by the back door until we came out, then start after us, grunting and trotting around headquarters. They were as loyal as dogs. We expanded their diet to table scraps, and they grew quickly. Their bristly hair came in, and pretty soon, petting them was like petting a wire brush. Javelinas, mistakenly called wild pigs, will never be contenders in the cute-and-cuddly category.

I named them Sandra and Ann after my sisters, but they looked so much alike that I never could tell which was Sandra and which was Ann. One would bump the other, trying to get in the lead. They would snort and play like they were going to fight, but they never did. When someone came to the ranch, I'd proudly introduce them. When people would ask which was Sandra and which was Ann, I'd say, "You decide."

Six months later, the twins took their first solo field trip. I walked out of the house. Only a handful of cats were milling around. For a moment, I couldn't put my finger on what was missing. Then, I realized Sandra and Ann weren't there. I went about my business half expecting them to show up, but they didn't return until sunset, when they trotted up and bumped my legs, eager for attention.

They hung around for a few more weeks, then disappeared. By the third day, I thought they had gone for good. But there they were, jogging across the grounds, back from some adventure. The duration of their visits shortened until they left never to return. I suspected that would happen. Still, I missed them—missed their antics, their loyalty, their affection. I never thought I would have javelinas as pets. But who was I to make that judgment? You can't always assume who your friends will or won't be. I liked to imagine they found some wild cousins and joined them in their travels. I hoped their journey turned out better than Bobby's.

CHAPTER 3

STORMY AND THUNDER

I was in Brownwood, Texas looking at some polled Hereford bulls raised by the Gill family. Years before, my dad had started buying bulls from Doc Gill, the patrón. DA felt they were some of the finest cattle in the West. Once a year during summer, I either drove a bobtail truck down to Brownwood, or Doc would ship a load of bulls to us on approval. Doc and I had just finished checking out the bulls he had selected for me. "Come on over to the barn," he said, pointing the way. "You've been such good customers, I want to give you a gift."

We walked the short distance to the barn and stepped inside. Doc headed over to the first stall. "Meet Stormy and Thunder," he said. Two Shetland ponies stood in the straw-covered space. They raised their heads, ears straight up, and eyed me curiously. "We've had these guys for years, but my kids are past the pony-riding age. I know you've got a few young 'uns at home."

I had never been around Shetlands, but I knew ranch kids and kids visiting ranches loved ponies. "Doc, wow, this is unexpected," I said. "It just so happens my nieces and nephews are spending most of the summer at Lazy B."

"Well then, I'll even throw in some saddles and bridles custom-made for these boys," said Doc. "You can stick 'em in the cab with you."

Doc had the ponies and bulls loaded on the truck. I thanked him again for the generous gift and began the thousand-mile road trip back to the ranch.

Just as I expected, the kids couldn't wait five minutes to ride Stormy and Thunder. My seven-year-old nephew quickly laid claim to Stormy. I saddled the pony and Barry climbed on. After much kicking and pulling and prodding and poking, he finally got Stormy to grudgingly go out the corral and up over the hill. About two minutes later, Stormy came running full-tilt back down the hill with Barry screaming in the saddle, holding onto the horn, both reins dragging on the ground. The only thing that stopped Stormy was the closed corral gate.

I ran up to the gate. "What happened?"

"I couldn't make this horse go," said Barry, sounding shaken. "I got off to get a little switch to help, and when I got back on, I dropped a rein, and he took off."

The war of the horses had begun. Stormy and Thunder responded like seasoned veterans. We quickly learned the Shetlands were uncooperative for almost anybody at any time. I could get them to bow to my wishes, but with riders who weren't strong enough or big enough or astute enough, they had their own way. It took so much effort to get them to haul you around, you'd rather walk. If they did start walking, or more likely running hell-bent back to the barn, they would scrape their rider on mesquite bushes or jump over gullies at such an odd angle, they'd lose their rider. Brian was clotheslined. He couldn't duck low enough; the line hit him in the neck, and he flopped to the ground. Jay got an ear partially torn off and needed it sewn back on after he was dumped. It became so bad, we started to laugh about it. The local doctor even took to saying, "Was this one of those ponies again?" By the end of the summer, those ponies were about as popular as chicken pox.

One day some friends came to visit and brought their son who probably was around six years old. The mother came to me and asked if he could ride one of the ponies down by the barn. Wanting to be a good host, I said sure, if I can lead your son, he can go for a ride. I saddled Thunder, and off we went out of the corral toward the hills with me leading. The entire way all I heard was: "Can I take the reins? I ride all the time." "Hey, let me take the reins." "Please, please, please give me the reins." The kid wore me down.

"Okay," I said. "Take the reins, but keep the horse pointed away from the barn. I'll walk behind you to make sure he doesn't run back to the barn in case he decides to turn around." I figured if I blocked the direct line back to the barn, Thunder wouldn't make an attempt to bolt. We started out and were doing fine until I took one step slightly off center. Thunder saw his opening. Quick as a flash, he ducked sideways, made a big circle, and got around me. He raced toward the barn like he was an NBA star headed for a dunk shot. The kid shrieked all the way back, but managed to hang on. He probably had the pee scared out of him. The monster had done his work. I was not happy, and by the looks of it, neither was his mother. From then on, those ponies never were ridden again.

Shortly after that, I changed our breed of cattle and never had occasion to buy more bulls from Doc Gill, which was fine by me. I didn't want to have to tell him that the ponies were great and we were happy to have them because we weren't. Sneaky mean hay burners—that's what those two ponies were. Their only goal in life was to get inside the barn and start munching hay. I did discover by asking other Shetland pony owners that my experience was not uncommon. I couldn't find anyone I disliked enough to re-gift those ponies to, so I kept them. The lesson learned? Sometimes it pays to look a gift horse in the mouth.

CHAPTER 4

NEIGHBORS

For as long as I could remember, the Donovan brothers lived on the property adjacent to the north side of Lazy B, on the banks of the Gila River. Rumor had it their family had moved from a polygamist Mormon colony down in Mexico. All three were tall and lean with a beard that extended part way down their bib overalls. During the warm months, they walked around barefoot. You'd think they were hillbilly mountain men, not cattle ranchers, but they ran a small herd of cattle, maybe twenty-five cows, on their ranch. They owned a horse, but were afraid to ride him.

If I recall, their names were Dick, Tim, and Tom, but the locals had taken to calling them Dim, Dimmer, and Blackout. Dim was the leader and the brightest of the three. He could read and write and if you met up with him, usually would comment on politics or county business. Dimmer and Blackout had never learned to read, and Blackout didn't even talk. They could be seen driving their old John Deere tractor pulling a two-wheeled flatbed trailer down the farm road to the town of Duncan. Their tractor was so old that it was the first model that used rubber tires. Dim drove, and Dimmer and Blackout rode on the trailer. Blackout wore a woman's stovepipe bonnet that stuck out in front of his face. When they walked into the store, they usually caused an outflow of customers who didn't appreciate their earthy odor. The owner never complained. The brothers didn't tarry and paid in cash. Along with their groceries, they bought their favorite food—Popsicles. At other times, if Dim and Dimmer had to go somewhere and they couldn't take Blackout with them, they would chain him to a tree so he couldn't wander off and get lost in the mesquites or wander onto the highway.

They lived in a two-room adobe shack without running water about a hundred yards from the river. The windows and doors never had screens so a horde of flies lived inside, along with chickens strutting around on the table and everywhere else. A pot of stew constantly simmered on the stove. I learned early on never to stop by at mealtime because they always offered to feed me. One helping of that thick, murky concoction was enough to last a lifetime. The locals called it "dog stew" because, as legend had it, if you dipped deep enough, you'd find the puppies at the bottom. No one ever admitted to taking a census of the local dogs. Probably a good thing.

When I came back to manage the Lazy B after graduating from college, I made it a habit to check in with the brothers from time to time to see if I could lend a hand in hauling their cows to auction. Since they had no way to get their cattle to market, they were glad to have my help. They always offered to pay me, but I always turned down the money. I don't believe in getting paid for doing something neighborly.

They had built a small corral out in the mesquite patch just past their house. That's where I picked up the cattle ready for sale. They had taken some mesquite limbs and tied them horizontally with bailing wire from one mesquite tree to another. They didn't use a lick of lumber. You had to look mighty close to identify it as a corral. If a calf wanted out, she could go to pushing against a limb and soon enough find herself on the other side.

Once, when I went to their place to see about hauling some calves to market, Dick, pleasant as always, asked me to take a look at one of his cows to see if he should cull and sell her. The brothers raised horned Herefords, which were cousins to the non-horned Herefords we raised on Lazy B. I followed Dick through the mesquites to the cow in question. I was flabbergasted. She was a rack of bones. Not only could I count every rib, I could have hung my hat on her hip bones, they stuck out so far. Her old horns were so long, they almost met in the middle.

"So what do you think? Should I sell her?" Dick looked at me seeking an answer.

"Well now," I said, trying to collect my senses, "if she were mine, I would certainly sell her. She probably won't bring a lot of money, though." He'd be lucky to get enough to buy a few boxes of Popsicles.

Dick replied, "Well, I thought you were going to tell me that. If I sell her, guess I should sell her mother too."

I couldn't reply for stifling a laugh. Lord, I never did see her mother. For all I know, she could have been standing behind a mesquite trunk, and I wouldn't have noticed her.

The brothers lived on their property until one of them died. I'm not sure who died. Maybe Dick. At any rate, the remaining two became frightened and went to live in a care facility.

It's easy not to notice how some people live, sometimes right under your nose. When you were around those three brothers, you were fully aware of the contrasts that life holds. Even in spite of their strange and disadvantaged lifestyle, they never mooched or infringed on us or took welfare from anyone. They were hardworking, honest men and good neighbors, and I'll always consider them my friends.

CHAPTER 5

A FERRARI ON FOUR LEGS

The new colt in the corral at Lazy B headquarters caught my eye. This particular colt had a larger build than his peers, with a broad chest, smooth barrel and muscular hips. The dark hair that most foals have at birth had been replaced by a shiny white coat, a dark stocking above each hoof, a black mane and tail, and a streak of black down his backbone. He explored his new territory, poking along the fence, his nose up and ears forward, and when the cowboys weren't holding class, nudged his more timid companions into games. The leader on the playground, he brought home a report card full of A's, though sometimes the teacher had to work at keeping his attention, which drifted if he learned the lesson quickly and became bored.

I felt an instant attraction, similar to what you feel when you meet someone you want to get to know better. Maybe it's the energy in the smile and eyes or the sweep of hands in conversation that make you want to start spending more time with that person. This little white guy fit that description. I could see him in my string of horses. I didn't need to claim him right then because he was headed out to Robb's Well for the next fifteen months or so. Throughout those months, I kept my eye on him.

The day he returned to the corral, I was waiting for him. Although he had not yet attained full stature, the muscles in his upper arms, forearms, and haunches had thickened, and the vertical space between his belly and the ground had lengthened. He had a smooth, effortless gait that exuded confidence. Based on his physique and coordination, I already could tell that he had the potential to be an athlete. I noted disappointment on the cowboys' faces when I said, "I'll take that white horse for my string."

He needed a better name than "that white horse." He reminded me of Robert E. Lee's famed white horse Traveller. I recalled seeing some photos of Lee mounted on his steed, dressed in full military regalia with a saber hanging at his side. Saber. Now there was a strong, steadfast word.

"Hey, you rascal," I said to him one morning, my arm extended over the fence. He trotted over for a pet. "You good with the name Saber? I'm thinking you can live up to it. What do you think?" He nudged his nose against my shoulder.

Saber and I began to get acquainted. Since he wasn't full-grown, and probably wouldn't be for another year, he couldn't do a hard day's work but could join me on less demanding days. Saber had an idea of what he wanted, and what he wanted didn't always agree with my bidding. Sometimes he could get a little prickly. He never bucked, but he didn't always cooperate. If I wanted him to turn right, he pulled left. If I rode him with spurs and touched him, and I rarely touched him, he'd look back and kick a hind foot at the spur or try to bite it, an especially annoying habit. By this point in my life, I was beginning to move away from the style of breaking a horse by breaking his will. Too often, this required punishing a horse severely. I had grown unwilling to settle for the consequence of having an unhappy horse.

One day, we were driving cattle from New Well to Lazy B headquarters, a six-mile trip. The previous two days of rounding up had been difficult, dusty work, but this was an easy day, so I opted to ride Saber. Jim Brister, our longtime cowboy, was pointing the cattle up front with another cowboy. The herd fanned out behind them. I brought up the drag in the back with the rest of the cowboys to show that I wasn't above doing drudgery work. I could see the whole show from there and could tell who was or wasn't carrying their load. Maybe Saber wanted to be in the lead or maybe he was bored. Whatever the issue, he was crankier than a teenager awakened from a sound sleep. I'd spur him along and he'd turn to bite me. It seemed like every hundred feet, I was pulling his head up and scolding him. I was getting annoyed at him being annoyed at me. That's when I saw Jim break from the lead and circle back toward me, something he wouldn't do unless he had to unload a piece of his mind.

He rode up next to me and gave Saber the once-over. "Alan, if I were on that damn horse, I'd draw that knot in your get-down rope and whip that thing against his sheath until he squealed for mercy." I held back a wince. The sheath protects a horse's penis and is a very sensitive area.

Saber's strong shoulders shifted rhythmically under my saddle, and a cow in front of us called out for her calf. I didn't want to argue with Jim or go against his judgment. I may have been the boss, but Jim was my senior and my mentor. For the first time in my life, I bucked his opinion. "I'm trying something a little different on him this time. I'm going to give him a chance to learn it on his own," I said.

Saber turned his head and jabbed his mouth at my spur. Large teeth flashed between curled lips. I yanked the reins, pulling his head back. Jim looked straight ahead and without a word, rode off.

"Damn it, Saber. Knock it off. What are you thinking?"

Saber jogged a few side steps. It was going to be a long day.

Not every day with Saber was long, and of course, I didn't ride him every day. Occasionally, he would be so interested in the task at hand that neither of us remembered I wore spurs. Within a few hours, though, he would bicker with me, and force me to dish out more patience and reaffirm my vow of training. More often than not, when Saber returned to the horse pasture for the night, and I slid off my boots and hung my hat, issues between us remained unresolved. Still, I babied him with extra grain, and he continued to grow.

About three months after Jim offered his advice, something happened. It was an unassuming day. Saber and I led a crew of cowboys to cut cattle for sale. The sun spilled over us, bright as always, and a mischievous breeze scrambled the desert dust with the sweat of men on horseback. We were nearing a late lunch when it hit me. On any other day, Saber would have tested me a dozen times by now. But here he was with his head and ears held high, so fully engaged in his job that I hadn't needed to reprimand or spur him once all morning. In fact, he had just moved a large steer to the outside of the herd with little direction from me. I had eyed the steer and thought okay, this guy needs to go. Maybe my hands had slightly, perhaps subconsciously, pulled the reins in the steer's direction, but maybe not. Maybe Saber read my mind. Regardless, he had moved the animal, slowly, gently, and before I knew it, had the steer in exactly the right spot at the edge of the herd. A new alertness tensed his body. I could feel us working together.

I said, "Wow, Saber, you've arrived." It was like what a hunter experiences the first time his dog points, waits for the shot, then perfectly retrieves the bird. By the time we returned to headquarters, I was sitting on a completely different horse. For whatever reason, Saber's resistance moved out and full cooperation moved in. From that day on, Saber became the best cow horse I ever rode. When we were out on the range, he seemed to know what I wanted to do. It was as if this athletic, smart companion could read my mind. I'd throw the saddle over him, chitchatting about the day like you would chat to your best friend. We then had the luxury of spending the entire day together, hanging out, running into challenges, having adventures. The line between work and pleasure dissolved.

About the same time, Saber did another extraordinary thing I've never had a horse repeat. One morning, the air cool against our faces, we set out at Saber's usual gait. I urged him to walk a little faster. I felt his gait change. He had broken into a running walk, the same gait as a Tennessee walking horse. No other horse on the ranch had such a gait, so he hadn't learned by imitating. His body naturally slipped into the pattern. I didn't even know how to respond except to enjoy the ride. It was like stepping off a tractor and into a Lexus.

"What the hell got into your horse? He just hit fourth gear. How'd you teach him that?" said Cole, pulling up beside me. His horse had to hit a long trot to keep up with Saber.

I shrugged my shoulders. "Good cowboys get the best out of their horses," I said. Three miles later, Saber wasn't even out of breath. The boss always sets the pace when riding out to the roundup, and cowboy culture says you never gripe about that pace. But that day the crew certainly looked disgruntled.

By the time Saber was five, he was so powerful and fast that when we worked cattle I always held him back a little. One day, curiosity got the better of me. I finished lunch before anyone else at the bunkhouse and didn't feel like shooting the breeze, so I headed outside to get a jump on re-saddling Saber. He was feeding with the other horses in the corral by the barn. That morning, we had herded four hundred cows and another two hundred calves into the large working lot at headquarters, and would spend the afternoon selecting and cutting cows and calves to sell. Any calves under six months would be branded and remain on the ranch.

I put my hand on Saber's neck and led him over to the saddle I had set on the ground. He looked like he was as eager to get out of the corral as I had been to get out of the bunkhouse. I could feel his muscles under my hand, relaxed but alert, ready for action. I threw the saddle on, cinched it, and settled on the worn leather like you settle in the driver's seat of a car. But this wasn't a minivan or pickup or souped-up SUV. Nor was it a Lexus or Infiniti or even a BMW or Mercedes.

This was a Ferrari.

I had never done an all-out test drive on Saber. Every day, I obeyed the speed limits. What would it feel like to pull on the Autobahn, shift into eighth gear, and let it go? It would be plain wrong never to answer that question. It was time to find out how truly fast my horse could run.

I walked Saber through the empty corrals and into the working lot. The cattle were in siesta mode, bunched in one end of the long corral. I spotted a big, old Brahman cow that I knew was fast.

"Let's give this gal a chase, Saber." Adrenaline revved my blood.

Saber knew what to do. He pushed her out of the bunch toward the back of the corral, close to the fence fortified with rows of double-barbed wire. The cow swung her head back and forth, irritated at having to move. Saber jump-started her into a sprint and took off after her. I let the reins go slack. He passed that cow like she was moving in slow motion, then pulled ahead of her to turn her back against the fence. He pivoted so hard, we angled to the ground, my elbow and shoulder skimming the dirt. My lower leg dragged across the ground. Before I knew it, we were sliding sideways across the soft surface, rocketing toward the barbed wire instead of alongside it. My leg was tucked under Saber's side, and I was still in the saddle. The barbed wire rose toward us like the wall of a racetrack rising toward the driver of an out-of-control car. But where a driver only has the traction of a slick track, we had the traction of soft earth. It slowed us down. When we stopped, I was in the saddle, but on my side, one leg under Saber, one on top. Other than Saber's weight compressing my trapped leg, nothing hurt. I lifted my head and assessed our predicament. Saber's legs had slid under the barbed wire, but he had miraculously stopped just before his belly made contact with it. I could see the surly wire inches above him, ready to attack at his slightest move and tear into him. The fear that he would try to scramble up gripped me.

"Saber, look, we're in a fix here," I said, trying to sound calmer than I felt. "It's not your fault your legs slid out from under you. I ran you too fast and turned you too hard." I rubbed his neck. "I'm the one to blame here. But right now, I need you to lay here real quiet and not struggle, because if you struggle, you're going to hurt yourself."

I kept petting him and talking to him, assuring him the other cowboys would be out soon. Saber didn't move one muscle. He just lay there like he was going to take a nap in the sun. I didn't dare dislodge my leg from under him, or slide out of the saddle. If you go down together, you stay down together. Besides, I knew someone would be headed our way soon. Funny how "soon" can feel like an entire afternoon.

Jim Brister was the first to arrive on horseback. "Looks like you got yourself in a helluva wreck here, Al," he said, throwing down one end of his rope. He waited for me to put the loop around my saddle horn, then dallied the rope on his saddle horn. Without a word, he turned his horse and started walking him. Saber and I slid out as smoothly as we had slid in. Saber lifted his head, pushed his feet into the ground, and snorted. I disengaged from the saddle as he hoisted himself up. Then I found my legs, brushed off the dirt stuck to my shirt, and readjusted my chaps and hat. Saber pawed a hoof at the ground as if scolding it for betraying him.

"No, Saber," I said. "I own this one, buddy. Blame me." I untied the rope and threw it back to Jim. I waited for the question to pop, the one that hung between us: What happened here? Jim merely recoiled the rope, hung it back on his saddle, and rode off. But under that black hat of his, I thought I saw a smirk.

By the time Saber was six years old, he reached his prime. Usually after our horses reached sixteen, seventeen, maybe eighteen years, we'd retire them from ranch work. Some of them went on to live until they were twenty or even twenty-five years. I didn't put it past Saber to be working cattle into his third decade. He was my number one horse and my best friend. If horses can be soul mates, Saber was mine. When I walked across the pasture in the dimness of dawn to catch him, he gave me a look that told me he was glad to see me and was ready to work. When we herded cattle, I almost could see his mind in action, planning out the next best play, and then with that innate gift of athletic coordination, putting it into action. We thought alike when it came to ranching. We embraced new experiences. Best of all, we respected each other one hundred percent. With mutual respect came true companionship and that magical bond of being best friends.

It was an early summer evening, when the sun sits a little longer in the sky. I had turned Saber out in the horse pasture and was at home in my office catching up on some bookkeeping before dinner. My mother came into the room, her face ashen, tears streaming down her face. She had been driving the Chrysler, returning from town, and was on the part of the main ranch road that ran through the horse pasture for a half-mile or so. When she rounded the bend, sunlight exploded in front of her, robbing her of vision. She didn't know which horse she hit until she got out of the car. There were five standing alongside the road, as they always were at that point in the pasture. One horse lay in the middle of the road. It was Saber. The impact broke his hind leg at the knee, the one place on a horse that can't heal.

One of my fast and hard rules is that I never ask someone to do something that I can't do myself. I have broken that rule only once in my life. I asked Cole Webb to put Saber down. I had put down his favorite dog some years back. I would not have been able to hold the gun steady nor see my target as anything but a blur through my tears. I was in the house when Cole honored my request, my mother and I holding each other, her seeking the forgiveness I already had given and me seeking solace. I'm not sure if I cried for two days or four or six. You never really stop crying over the loss of a loved one. Nor do you stop loving. Love is kind of like the sun. It can be warm and gentle, nourishing every part of you; other times, it shines harsh and hard and it burns. But there's no way to avoid the sun. It appears over the horizon every day and brings with it hardships, heartbreaks, adventures, joys, and even though we may not always see it, love.

~PART 2~

ON INNOVATION

Life is simpler when you plow around the stump.

CHAPTER 6

LEARNING TO FLY

I was getting dang tired of the nine-hour drive. It seemed like every week I had to do something for the Cattleman's Association or the Farm Bureau or one of the other boards I'd been roped into serving on, and those somethings had to be done in Phoenix, the hub of Arizona. One morning, I woke up especially tired. It occurred to me that an airplane would make these trips a bunch easier. I wasn't in love with the idea of flying, but I was ready to be divorced from midnight drives. The ranch already had a landing strip that was used by cow buyers or pilot friends.

My brother-in-law Gene was a flight instructor at Luke Air Force Base in Phoenix, so I asked him to keep his eyes open for a small plane. "Nothing fancy," I said. "Just something to get me from here to there and use around the ranch."

Within a few months he called. "Found a nice little single-engine Piper Tri-Pacer," Gene said. "Maybe you better come over and have a look." I didn't know a Tri-Pacer from any other Pacer, but the next morning, my pickup and I hit the road.

Gene had arranged for us to take a test flight with the plane's owner at Scottsdale Airport. We walked up to the tiny bird and my first thought was I'd have to fold up to fit in it. I reached out to touch it. The owner flinched. "Watch it there. You don't want to poke through that fabric," he said. So much for planes being made of aluminum. The three of us climbed in with me, the only non-pilot, in the back and Gene in the pilot's seat. He taxied to the runway, took off, and started circling the city. I could tell he was asking the owner questions, but I couldn't hear anything over the engine's roar.

"Nice little plane, Al," he said after landing. Gene said maintenance records indicated the motor was good and probably would get another five hundred hours before requiring an overhaul.

I turned to the owner. "How much do you want for it?"

"Let's call it thirty-five hundred."

I asked him for a pen and wrote out a check. At the time I wasn't tuned into thinking about insurance or an annual inspection or any other due diligence typically done at the point of sale. Guess that's why he looked surprised when I handed him the check, but he willingly handed over the title and the logbooks. He then showed me the space in the hangar he had rented. I was hoping to get a flying lesson on the spot, but Gene had to return to Luke to teach some classes and would be tied up all week. Rather than drive back to Lazy B, I decided to spend the night with Sandra and her husband John, who lived in Phoenix at the time.

The next morning I headed back to the airport. I wanted to fiddle around with the plane and get to know it a bit. Using the tow bar, I pulled the Piper out of the hangar, disconnected the bar and stowed it in the back of the plane where it had been when Gene flew. Once in the pilot's seat, I found the brake under the dash and messed around with the steering wheel, turning it right, then left. I noticed a starter button just waiting to be pushed. Three quick turns of the propeller and the engine fired. As long as it was revved up, I figured I'd better do some taxiing. I discovered when I mashed the left pedal on the floor, the plane turned left; when I mashed the other, it swerved right. I taxied around the airport, getting the feel for how the plane felt on the ground. It all seemed pretty easy. Heck, I thought, maybe I should just fly the bird. Good Sense intervened and said that I needed instruction.

So I made a deal with Good Sense. The deal was that I would pull up to the administration building, and if an instructor were just waiting for a student, I'd be that student, and if there were no instructor, I'd fly by myself. I pulled up, set the brake, and hoofed it inside. By golly, who was sitting behind the desk but Tony Baldwin, my old fraternity brother. We had played hours of poker and bridge together at the University of Arizona and shared more than a few beers. Turns out he was the manager of the airport and a flight instructor.

"So what brings you this way?" Tony said after we had caught up on where life had taken us since bridge games and Budweiser.

"I just bought that Piper sitting out there," I said.

"I didn't know you were a pilot, Al."

I hesitated. I've always been proud of telling the truth. "Well, I've flown a bit, but never piloted a Tri-Pacer. Guess I better get checked out. Make sure I know what I'm doing."

"Great! You caught me at a slack moment," said Tony, slapping his legs and standing up. "Let's go fly."

Next thing I knew we were strapped in our seats.

Tony pointed to a runway and said, "Taxi over there." I steered the plane just like I had been doing all morning.

Tony grabbed the pre-flight checklist off the dash. "Let's go down the list," he said. I felt like I was taking a test in school with a teacher who assumed I had read the chapter, but the only thing that I had read was the title. "Looks like you have plenty of fuel," he said. "Now check the mags."

I noticed a keyhole below the word "MAGS" and turned the already inserted key as far as it would go. The engine started to sputter. I quickly flipped the key back and the engine purred again.

Tony frowned. "You only want to check one mag at a time—left mag, then right mag. Make sure you don't turn both off like that or you might damage the engine." He returned the checklist to the dash. "Final thing—drop one notch of flaps." While teaching myself to taxi, I had pulled the handle that maneuvered the flaps. At that time, Scottsdale didn't have a radio-controlled field, so Tony's "give it the throttle and let's go" was all the permission I needed.

I pointed the plane down the runway, pushed in the throttle, and followed Tony's advice not to pull back on the wheel. It was a rare windless day. The little plane took itself off and started flying. This is too easy, I thought.

Tony crossed his arms. "Turn left and get out of the pattern. We'll get into the practice area and do some turns," he said. Turning a Tri-Pacer is about as difficult as turning a car into a parking space. A few quick miles and we arrived in the practice area. When does the hard stuff start? I wondered.

Tony proceeded to give a series of commands. Climb to and maintain twenty-four hundred feet. Turn left. Turn right. Climb a hundred feet. Descend two hundred feet. "Now pull the nose up and stall it," said Tony. I did just that. The plane shook and the nose dropped, then straightened out and resumed flying speed. Somehow I knew it was going to do that. Man, I was on track to ace this course.

"Okay, head back and we'll shoot a few landings."

With no wind, it was easy to line up the plane with the runway's centerline. "Pull back to twenty-two," Tony said, pointing at the manifold pressure gage. "We'll go in at eighty." I pulled the throttle and sure enough, the needle dropped from twenty-seven to twenty-two, and the plane slowed to eighty miles per hour. The nose was pointed down and the ground was coming up to meet us pretty fast. I knew I had to pull back on the wheel to level off, a maneuver I later learned is called rounding out. The problem was I didn't know when to round out, so I never did.

The plane hit the runway with a boom and bounced like a basketball thirty feet in the air. Tony's arms came unglued. He grabbed the wheel on his side, which happened to be higher than mine since my side was dipping at a crazy angle. Suddenly, my thick head realized I had no idea what I was supposed to do. Were we in control or out of control? I looked down at the runway below. It looked hard. Tony straightened the plane and proceeded to land it.

"Damn, Al! That was a really bad landing."

Practicing my pilot coolness, I said, "Tony, that's the worst landing I've ever made."

"Well, give it the power and try again. Maybe you'll do better next time."

I flew back into the pattern, came around, lined up the plane, and headed down. I pulled back on the wheel, rounding out in time to make the landing passable.

"Again," said Tony.

After three more landings, each of which was better than the last, Tony decided that was enough for one day. We started taxiing back to the hangar. By this time, I began to recognize the error of my ways. I needed instruction, which meant the only way out of this mess was to confess my sins.

"Tony," I said, invoking brotherly love. "I've never flown before."

Tony looked at me, his eyes wide. "What did you just say?"

I repeated.

He must have been seeing blood because his face turned bright red. "Stop this plane. Right here." We were still on the tarmac and two hundred yards from the hangar. I pulled on the brake and stopped the plane. Tony opened the door, jumped out and stalked off without a word or glance back.

Shit, I thought, this was a helluva dumbass attack. Here I am with a plane, no license, and a mad instructor. What's an idiot cowboy to do now? I taxied back to the hangar, hauled out the tow bar, and stowed the plane. I knew I had to go see Tony. I got in my pickup and drove to the administration building.

Tony used more swear words than I'd ever heard in the frat house. He was so angry, he shook. Can't say I blamed him. I finally had to pull out my trump card. "Hey, man, brothers can't stay angry with each other," I said. "Come on, let's go out and I'll buy us some beers." I think it was the promise of free beer that convinced him to agree.

About a case of beer later, Tony said, "You'd better come back tomorrow and get some more instruction or you'll kill yourself." He also told me to buy a logbook and a student pilot license.

The sun was halfway to noon when I arrived at the airfield, logbook and license in hand. I strapped into the plane with new, humbled respect. Tony, still snippy but now with a hangover, climbed in and told me to shoot three touch-and-goes. After the third he said, "Take me back to the hangar, and you shoot some landings." My heart jumped and landed in my throat. My lifeline was severed; it was solo time. Up to this point, I had accumulated ninety minutes of instruction.

I did as I was told. I was too intent on trying to make it all work to be frightened. After the third landing, I taxied to get Tony's critique. "You passed," he said. "Now take that damn plane and get off this property. I don't want to see you anymore."

"But Tony, I don't have any place to take it."

"I thought you told me you had a strip at your ranch."

"I do."

"Well, then take it home."

"How do I do that?"

"Fly it, for chrissakes."

"But how do I navigate? I have no idea—"

"You came here on the highway, didn't you? So follow the goddamn highway home."

Tony turned his attention to his desk and refused to say another word.

Holy Jesus, I thought, I'm way over my head here. I couldn't think of anything else to do but fly my little bird to Lazy B. Fortunately, it was another windless day. I took off, and did what Tony suggested: I followed the highway. For two hundred miles, questions tormented me. What if the wind kicks up? What if there's a crosswind when I land? How high do I fly? How far will a tank of fuel go? What if the motor quits? By the time I set the plane down on the ranch's dirt airstrip, I was used up. I knew my next step was to enroll in flight school.

I contacted Bill Woods, an instructor I knew in Safford, Arizona, sixty miles west of Lazy B. If I flew down, he'd give me some instruction. After a half-dozen lessons, he suggested I schedule a test with Kenny Switzer, an FAA flight examiner in Deming, New Mexico. I ordered the material for the written part of the exam, studied it, then scheduled a test date.

Kenny looked at my logbook and scratched his head. "I've never seen a logbook like this. You're pretty far from the forty hours I usually require." I didn't say a word. "Well, you came all this way. Let's get in and see if you can fly."

The written and flight tests were rigorous but I managed to leave Deming with a pilot's license. I ended up flying that little bird five hundred hours and became a real pilot. It was a serviceable little airplane that I never had any trouble with whatsoever. Every time I flew, I kept one eye on the ground, always aware of where I could land if in trouble and always thinking that I was one lucky son of a gun to be alive.

CHAPTER 7

STUCK IN THE WASH

If memory serves me, I was thirteen, and the month of August was dwindling. It was a warm day with a few clouds hanging out in a bright blue sky. Rastus, one of our long-time cowboys, had put a sick bull in the small holding pasture near the corral at New Well. He suggested we go get him. New Well was a good twenty miles northwest of headquarters, too far to drive a sick bull, so I saddled one of the broncs I had been training on all summer and loaded him in our rickety four-horse trailer. I'd need him to get the bull into the corral at New Well. Rastus and I hitched the trailer to the pickup, then Rastus recruited one of our hands to drive because Rastus didn't drive. Our foreman Leroy and I hopped in the old jeep we kept around for traveling over tough terrain. With its four-wheel drive, it could plow through just about anything.

Getting to New Well wasn't the easiest proposition because of the roads—or lack thereof. For a good part of the way, we could take the highway that ran east and west through the ranch. Three miles before the highway entered Duncan, we would have to turn south onto a five-mile dirt road. It was the road from hell. The clay soil was pretty much the worst soil on the entire ranch. It was like fine silt, so soft that even a slight breeze could kick it up. When it rained, it drank up all the water and turned into a slick mud bog. The summer monsoon had dumped some rain during the month at headquarters, but not too much at New Well.

Sure enough, when we arrived, dust was blowing a foot or so above the road. The jeep plunged ahead, but the pickup, well, we held our breath hoping that the wheels wouldn't start spinning and dig in, stopping the truck dead in its tracks. We made it the five miles without incident and pulled into the pasture. I unloaded the bronc and soon found the bull. He looked pretty droopy. It was a slow walk to the corral. Once there, he didn't want anything to do with the trailer. The cowboys and I worked with him for a good thirty minutes trying to get him to willingly step into it. Finally, all four of us grabbed him and pulled and pushed, pushed and tugged and got him loaded in the front part of the trailer. We loaded the bronc into the back part.

While we were struggling with the bull, some big black clouds appeared and had grown bigger and blacker. As we headed out of New Well, huge raindrops started to fall. Before we had driven five hundred yards, the clouds decided to release their catch. Rain descended in sheets. The jeep didn't have a cover and we hadn't brought our slickers, so instantly Leroy and

I were soaked to the bone. And so was the road. We had come in on a cloud of dust and were going out across a puddle of slick mud. Pretty soon, I turned around and saw the pickup's wheels spinning in place. We kept a chain in the back of the jeep in case a vehicle got stuck. Leroy said, "You better get out and hook that chain up."

I got down on my knees in the mud and hooked it to the frame. Leroy hit the gas and pulled the pickup out of the mud. A half-mile later, it got stuck again. Out I went. Before I could hook the chain, lightning started to fall. More lightning than I had ever seen. It popped everywhere. I watched a bolt hit so close I could see the dust it kicked up from below the layer of mud. Thunder crashed and shook the ground. Again, the jeep pulled the pickup out and our caravan plowed through the thickening mud, slipping and sliding. Lightning flashed in front of us, behind us, all around us. I was one teenage boy scared out of his wits. I kept hoping that we could make it out before the rain had a chance to sink deeper into the soil, making the road impassable.

It didn't take long for the heavy pickup to get stuck again. I jumped out onto the slippery mud, holding the chain and fearing that any second I might light up like a Christmas tree. All I could think of was the saddle hanging in the barn at headquarters. It was the only remains of a cowboy and his horse, both killed by lightning back in the early days of Lazy B. I had grown up fascinated by the many small holes in it. I wasn't finding this light show quite so fascinating.

I hooked the chain to the pickup and hopped back into the jeep. Leroy gunned the motor so hard I thought we'd pull the pickup's frame apart. But we got it out. Again it got mired in mud. It happened so many times, we started to wonder if we would make it to Railroad Wash before it flooded. Railroad Wash was the last hurdle to cross before reaching the highway. It drained about one hundred fifty square miles of land and when full, turned into a raging river one hundred feet wide and six feet deep with a current strong enough to carry away a jeep or pickup. If we didn't make it across, we would be stuck there for hours. We were in a race against water.

We finally arrived at the wash. The water was moving fast, but it still looked low enough to cross. We made the decision to again hook the chain to the back of the jeep and the front frame of the pickup. Leroy would drive the jeep as fast as possible into the wash; we hoped its momentum would carry it, the pickup, and trailer across the water and up the embankment. Leroy floored it. We bounced into the wash and splashed through the water. The jeep was halfway up the embankment when it came to a dead halt in thick mud. The pickup stopped. It had started up the embankment, but the trailer remained in the wash. Water gushed around its tires. Lightning dropped around us.

Leroy kept gunning the motor. The tires spun in the mud, digging deeper and deeper into the embankment. It looked like we were going to have to leave the pickup and trailer and save the jeep. I hopped out of the jeep. An enormous pain shot through my foot. For a moment, I thought lightning had hit the bottom of my boot. I'm sure the cowboys heard me yell over the thunder. I turned my boot over. A big mesquite thorn had punctured it and was well into my foot. No wonder it hurt like hell. I tried to pull it out, but my hands were so wet, I only managed to break it off at the sole of my boot. The rest of that sucker stayed in my foot. I hobbled to the back of the jeep.

I unhooked the chain, and Leroy gunned the jeep up the embankment to flat ground. Right away, I could tell the chain wasn't long enough to reach the pickup. I looked up the wash. Between the torrents of rain, I could see the draw a quarter mile up filling with water. I limped into the wash and sloshed to the back of the trailer. I could get the horse out, but the bull was lying down, looking like he wasn't going to go anywhere, flood or no flood.

In my world, DA was the absolute boss and tyrant and would never forgive me for losing pickup, trailer, horse, and bull. That was unthinkable. But it was about to happen. Even though I was the youngest of our group, the failure would rest squarely on my shoulders. I couldn't even wrap my mind around that one. If I had to carry that damn pickup out on my back, I would do it. I hobbled out of the wash to consult with Leroy.

That's when I noticed the nylon saddle rope under his seat. It had been there for some time. One of the strands had broken on it, and the cowboys assumed it was no good. Most of them relied on hemp ropes, but I had seen a hemp rope bust in half when too much torque was applied. Though the nylon rope was only three-eighths of an inch wide, it was thirty feet long. I grabbed it. Just maybe we could use it to lengthen our towline. I didn't really believe that this worn out rope had enough strength to not break, but I had no other choice. It was panic time.

There wasn't even time to have a board meeting. I shoved one end of the rope at Leroy and told him to tie it to the jeep's hitch. I tied the other end to the chain still hooked to the pick up frame. I gave Leroy the signal and he hit the gas. The nylon started to stretch and stretch and stretch. It must have stretched six feet. I expected it to bust at any second. The jeep fishtailed and slid, but Leroy kept gunning it. Lo and behold, the pickup started to move. An inch, a foot, then a little faster. I started hopping up and down on one foot and cheering everyone on. Little by little, here came the pickup and trailer up the muddy side of the wash, then onto flat ground. Two minutes later, the water was so deep that it would have swept the pickup and trailer away had they still been in the wash. The pickup would have floated away to the Gila River and ended up buried in the sand, its tires poking up like gravestones.

Muddy and soaked, the four of us regrouped, reclaimed our dignity, then drove to the highway. By the time we pulled into headquarters, the rain had almost stopped. We unloaded the horse and bull into the corral. I went into the barn, found some pliers, gritted my teeth, and pulled the thorn out of my foot. We never told DA the details of our journey. He wouldn't have been impressed. We only told a very sanitized version of what happened. Gee, the road was a little slick on the way out, and we had to tie on the chain in a few places to get the pickup through those sticky spots. In fact, none of us ever discussed it again, even with each other. We didn't figure ourselves heroes. We figured we were lucky to have survived. The bull must have been grateful to be alive, too. He recovered from his ailment and ended up living many more years, happily fulfilling his siring role at the ranch.

CHAPTER 8

FORTY QUAIL FOR SISTER SANDRA

When I was ten years old, my sister Sandra was a law student at Stanford. She regularly wrote letters to us about all the happenings in her world, and MO would read them at the dinner table. I had never been to Stanford, but I knew Sandra lived with nineteen other female students in graduate housing.

One day, we received a letter saying that soon it would be Sandra's turn to prepare dinner for her fellow residents. She thought it would be wonderful to cook quail, two birds per woman. Lazy B had thousands of quail. My folks agreed that it was a good idea, but they weren't about to capture forty quail.

I thought, golly, here's my chance to make a difference in a way I'd never done before. Sandra lived in a world that seemed as far away as the moon. But to hear my dad talk about it, well, he had so much reverence for Stanford, probably because he was ready to go there when he was drafted into World War I. He never did fight. Nor did he ever attend Stanford. But he repeatedly told us kids that Stanford was the best college in the nation, and it was a real honor to graduate from there. I couldn't help Sandra do that, but I could help her with her dinner. It was a golden opportunity to do something that no one else would or could do.

I had a shotgun and knew how to use it, but DA said that he didn't want to send quail with buckshot in them. That meant that I would have to capture the birds. I had done this in the past, but I only needed to catch enough to feed our family of four. That, in itself, took a full day to do. With a goal of catching forty quail, I had to put my little thinker on and calculate logistics and coordinates. We didn't have a freezer, but the birds would keep in the refrigerator at least three or four days. DA said we could get the birds packed in dry ice at the icehouse in Lordsburg and then ship them to Palo Alto.

It was winter, and we had just harvested a bunch of grain called hygaria. Quail go crazy for the heads of hygaria. We had hauled full stalks out to the corral headquarters for cattle feed, and coveys of quail flocked to share in the spoils. We had five different coveys that freeloaded at the headquarters, with up to twenty or thirty birds per covey. The coveys tended to arrive around eight o'clock in the morning and two and four o'clock in the afternoon. I gave myself three days to catch forty quail.

I got busy and started inventing traps. First, I built three rectangular boxes. I nailed together some two-by-four pieces of lumber to make the sides and covered the tops with chicken wire. For the first trap, I made a figure four trigger, then propped one end of a box on it. Inside the box, I placed handfuls of hygaria. The trick was to lure the quail under the angled box. When enough quail were under it, one of them would trip the trigger, and the box would fall, hopefully on ten or twelve birds.

For the second trap, instead of using a trigger, I dug a small ditch with a trowel. I placed the box halfway over the ditch, then put grain around the ditch, in the ditch, and under the box. The game plan was for the quail to follow the grain trail down into the ditch and up into the box. Once the quail were in the box, I'd have to hightail over and move it before the quail escaped back through the ditch.

The third trap was the one I liked best. It had a trigger that was a six-inch block of wood with a long string tied to it. I made a hay bale fort in the hay lot and made sure to be out there directly after breakfast when the birds started showing up. I'd hide behind the bales, string in hand, and peek out at their twittering heads. Soon enough I'd be feeling lucky at all the happy birds pecking at the grain. When eight or ten had found their way under the box, I'd yank the string and see just how lucky I was.

I quickly learned that no matter which trap I used, I had to keep moving it. Those quail were smart. They saw their buddies get trapped and would avoid the space where the trap was set. If I moved the trap ten or twenty feet away, they didn't seem to recognize the box and would hunker under it to peck at the grain.

The next trick was to get them out from under the box. I took a piece of stiff wire and made a hook. I'd lift the box a little and hook a quail leg. At first, I lost quite a few birds, but then I got real good at catching them. As soon as the bird was out, I'd pull its head off. I was maybe the best quail trapper I had ever seen. Then again, I didn't have much competition.

My mother wouldn't let me bring the quail inside before they were cleaned and washed, so each day I field-dressed them outside. As I handed them over, she put them in a bucket of salt water and stored the bucket in the frig. In three days, I had my forty quail.

DA and I took them to the icehouse in Lordsburg, then to the nearby Texas Arizona Freight. Those birds had a two-day express truck ride all the way to Palo Alto.

I couldn't wait for Sandra's next letter. It came and thanked us for sending the quail. It was the best dinner that anyone at the house had ever fixed. Sandra sounded quite proud of the dinner, but no one was more proud of it than I. I had set my goals, reached them, and touched a world that I didn't know, full of people who I would never meet. That was one cool deal.

CHAPTER 9

GENTLED CATTLE

DA was a rancher who preferred to ranch on foot instead of on the back of a horse. During spring and fall roundups, cowboys on horseback would drive a herd of cattle into the corral, and he would have them off their horses faster than lightning hits the ground. Those boys practically ran their legs off opening and closing gates and getting the cattle settled. Of course, they bitched. I walked in different boots. I'd been raised around cowboys like Jim Brister who practically lived on a horse, and like Jim, I loved working horseback.

When I took over Lazy B, roundups had more running than a tri-state track meet. Because our cattle weren't accustomed to seeing a man on a horse, they had become increasingly ornery and wild, and they spooked when you rode up to them in the pasture. With pastures as big as eighty square miles, the herd had a fine time playing hide and seek with us.

My real wake-up call to the problem came one spring during roundup. The cowboys and I spent two hard days gathering heifers out of the Cottonwood pasture where they had spent the past year maturing to adulthood. We finally got them in the corrals at headquarters, a temporary holding spot. The next day I instructed a handful of cowboys to drive half the herd up into the black hills where they would join the main cow herd. I should have appointed one of the hands to take up the lead and set the pace, but I didn't. The cowboys all hung out at the back of the bunch. They told me later that when the group started the two-thousand-foot climb up the rocky canyon, the heifers charged so fast that the cowboys couldn't catch them to slow them down. Three heifers ran themselves to death and died right in the middle of the canyon. I was horrified. I was not going to be a rancher who killed cows by running them to death. I resolved to make major changes in how we handled the cattle.

One way was to invest in more cowboys and faster horses. But that continued to promote unwanted commotion and distress to the animals. Another way was to bait the cattle with feed, a common practice among ranchers. During the year the heifers lived in the pasture growing from six-month-old calves to eighteen-month-old cows, we could go out with a truck, honk the horn, and spread a trail of corn or hay. Over time, the cattle would recognize the sound of the blaring horn, associate it with food and not get all jittery. That didn't address the imminent problem. Cowboys on horseback would still incite panic, and off we would be at the races. What we really needed to do was get the cattle to change their perception of us. Exactly how to do that was the question.

I decided the next time we weaned calves, we would put them through an intensive gentling program while they were still in the headquarter corrals. Get them to recognize us. The cowboys thought my marbles had bounced on the ground and gotten buried in the dust. But the boys wanted their paychecks. So while we weaned that next group of calves, three cowboys and I saddled up, went into the corral, and talked to those babies. Real calm, real friendly.

We held the group of a hundred and fifty in a corral corner, then started driving them down the side. Of course, they broke and ran all over the place, so we gathered them again, all the while chatting like we were best friends. Every time we tried to drive them, they'd scatter. Twenty minutes later, the calves were pooped. We gave them a break, but came back three more times that day and repeated the drill. After four or five days, the training started to stick. The calves began to follow a man on horseback. They no longer feared us. If a calf left the group, one of the cowboys would race after her and bring her back to the herd. The lesson learned? If you go off on your own, life is uncomfortable; if you stay with the herd, life is good. Pretty soon they got to following the lead horse around the corral, then through the gate, and out to an adjoining small pasture. It was an exercise in repetitive teaching, like teaching kindergarteners to stay in a line and file into the classroom. By the time we turned those cattle out for the year, they were the best-behaved bunch on the ranch. But we still didn't have proof the training would hold.

The time came to gather them. I took a full crew out not knowing what to expect because those heifers hadn't seen us on horseback for a year. During the past twelve months, we periodically drove out in a pickup to check on them. We made sure the windmill was pumping water and restocked their salt supply if necessary. They were accustomed to seeing vehicles, not horses. In the past, when we rode horseback, the cattle would see us a half-mile away, rev their jets, and bolt. This time, we got to the half-mile mark, spread out ready for action, and those cows? They didn't lift a head. A quarter mile, and all was calm. I was about ready to fall off my horse. We were right around the herd before some of those heifers finally glanced up as if to say, "Oh hello, it's you." So I said right back to them, "Hey girls, glad to see you. Glad you waited for us." The cowboys defaulted into their mode for rounding up gentled cattle, and the day ended without a hitch.

What surprised me even more is that when the babies of those heifers grew up, they weren't afraid of us either. Their mamas had done the cowboys' job. Training became twice as easy. The whole program fed on itself and little by little, year by year, required less energy. We had next to no runaways. The success still warms me. I had shaken the dice and thrown them on the table. Lucky me. They had come up a seven. Herd behavior modification training, I called it.

Cowboys, neighbors, friends, and colleagues all hailed from Missouri when I told them the gentling cattle story. One neighbor south of Lazy B had the wildest bunch of cattle that time and time again ran away. After each incident, this frustrated rancher would pound in a piece of fence along the getaway trail in an attempt to contain the animals. Pretty soon he had the most nonsensical fencing ever created. I went to him and explained the program, how it was foolproof, and how he could do it. "That's a bunch of shit," he said.

No one outside Lazy B ever bought into the program, but I never stopped using it. I knew a good thing when I had it. Pays to keep your mind and your eyes open. You never know what you might find that makes life better for yourself and those around you.

CHAPTER 10

FIFTEEN HUNDRED WILD HORSES

My life seems to have run on the spur railroad line more often than the main line. So it went the day I made an offer on a thirty-five-thousand-acre ranch in the Sand Hills of South Dakota. I definitely didn't need this ranch. At the time, I was wearing the wings off my plane managing two ranches, the Lazy B and the Rex Ranch, a forty-five thousand acre spread in Nebraska. Between the two, I was running four thousand mother cows. I was cattled out. So why did I buy a third ranch? Ever hear of love at first sight? The minute I set eyes on that lush grass, those towering trees, wild turkeys, pheasants, ponds, a creek, a river, I tumbled head over heels. The problem was I had no idea what I was going to do with that gorgeous sea of grass.

I hadn't even closed on the property when fellow rancher and horse lover Dayton Hyde gave me the lowdown on the plight of our country's wild horses. He said the Bureau of Land Management was culling the horses from government lands when the herds grew too large and overgrazed the grasses. Helicopters buzzed them into makeshift corrals. From there, they were transported to feedlots. Families were split. They had no room to run. Dayton said some horses were so bored they would eat each other's tails and manes. Most of the pretty wild horses went into public adoption programs, while the old, the scarred, the one-eyed were destined to spend the rest of their days in horse prison. This was 1988. About two thousand horses were in captivity in various feedlots around the West, not the forty thousand that some three decades later are in captivity.

Before Dayton finished his horror story, a crazy idea grabbed me. Maybe, just maybe, I could turn the South Dakota ranch into a sanctuary for government-owned wild mustangs. The horses would regain their freedom, and the government would have a hands-on caretaker. A few days later, I pitched the idea to the BLM. The higher-ups cautiously shared my excitement, but said that Congress, the BLM's boss, would need to authorize the deal. So Dayton and I donned our cowboy hats and boots and made a lobbying trip to Washington D.C. With the help of Arizona's Senator Dennis DeConcini, Congress attached a rider to a bill that gave me the green light to take fifteen hundred imprisoned wild horses, put them on the best piece of land those animals had ever seen, and keep them happy for the rest of their lives. That's when I poured myself a stiff scotch. I knew horses, but I'd never worked with wild horses, and I was about to get a whole bunch of them.

I had to get the ranch in shape. I had bought it on foreclosure and it badly needed repairs. I flew up some workers from Arizona and set them to mending pasture fences, building up corral fences, and painting the barn and main house. I contracted a local company to drill more wells in the pastures, and I spread phosphorous on the hay meadows. It would make more and better hay for the horses, and we needed a plentiful supply to get them through the blizzards of winter. By the time the horses started arriving, Mustang Meadows Ranch was spit-polished and ready to receive them. But was I?

I knew from talking to cowboys who worked in one of the Nevada feedlots that wild horses feared humans more than any other creature. Rightly so. The humans who professed to love them did nothing but traumatize them. As a result, when the wild horses noticed a cowboy on horseback heading toward them, they bolted in the opposite direction. This did not bode well for Mustang Meadows Ranch or me. My motto always has been to leave the land healthier than how I found it. Horses are rough on land. A large herd can quickly overgraze a pasture that can take years to repair itself. The big question hanging in the humid South Dakota air: Could I make friends with a large herd of wild mustangs and train them to follow a cowboy on horseback through gates and into fresh pasture? During the summer, I would need to move the horses almost weekly. If they weren't trained, they would jump fences and scatter across two counties. The only thing I knew to try was the herd modification program that I used on cattle. The horses started arriving in mid-September. We had until May tenth of the following year, the day summer grazing officially began in that part of the world, to get them trained.

The roping arena next to the barn became the training arena. It was one hundred fifty feet by five hundred feet. I decided to train one hundred horses at a time. During the first training session, the frightened horses gathered at one end of the arena, shaking their heads and whinnying nervously. Three cowboys and I mounted our horses and rode into the opposite end of the arena.

"Let's spread out and take it at a walk," I said. "No quick movements. Just ride toward the group." The men, all professional horse handlers, nodded. "And at the same time, we're going to talk to them. Out loud. Real friendly-like."

The cowboys looked at me like I was crazy, but they followed the game plan. We were about halfway down the arena, all talking in soothing voices, when one of the horses charged away from the group and started a stampede. Horses raced by us. As abruptly as the stamped started, it ended, with the horses bunched in the opposite corner. The cowboys and I turned our horses and repeated the drill. Again and again, we repeated. After twenty minutes, the horses started looking harassed.

"Let's give them a break, boys," I said.

We returned to the barn to unsaddle. That's when I told the guys that I'd see them back in two hours. Now they looked at me baffled. I reminded them it was all about repetition. Building trust through repetition. Little did the cowboys know repetition would mean every two hours, every day until the horses agreed to do what we wanted them to do. I had no idea how many days that would take.

Turned out the mustangs' behavior changed significantly after about four or five days of intensive training. They realized that we weren't like other men who had chased them with helicopters and forced them into corrals. They began looking at us as the alpha males. The next lesson they learned was to follow a cowboy around the arena without running past him. Then, they learned to follow their cowboy leader through a gate. After that, the cowboy would lead them through grassy lanes separating pastures. Their last exercise was to follow the cowboy around a small pasture as a group, with none bolting or running ahead.

Except for Thanksgiving and Christmas, the cowboys and I trained the horses every day from fall through winter and into spring. Once one hundred horses graduated from training school, we started training another one hundred. The trained horses were kept in a pasture, while the untrained horses remained in corrals. As the program began to work, the cowboys began to believe in it.

Finally, May arrived and the big move to summer grazing was about to happen. Twelve hundred wild horses now lived at Mustang Meadows. We needed to move all of them from the small pastures near headquarters, across open range to the large pasture at Mud Lake. The six-mile trek was the litmus test of our training and the backbone of the sanctuary's success. Would the horses stick together or would they spread out across the open range and disregard what we had taught them?

On the morning of May tenth, I was a bundle of nerves. Seven of us rode into the heifer pasture where the horses were grazing. I'll always remember their scent, that strong pungent smell of wildness. When they saw us coming, they shook their heads and threw snorts into the spring breeze. Our group spreading across the pasture told them that some drama was about to unfold and they were to be part of it. They stomped and called for each other, then began to gather into one large herd.

I looked down the line of riders, checking our formation. At a measured pace, we swept around the pasture. The leaders of the herd felt the gentle pressure and moved toward the corner where the gate led into the next pasture. The foreman and I peeled away from the line and galloped in front of the leaders to set the pace. We rode side by side about twenty feet apart. The lead horses were so close to us that we could hear their rhythmic breathing. Like a rope uncoiling, the herd began to string out and lengthen. The forty-eight hundred hooves beating the sandy soil sounded like the muted thunder of Indian drums. The sound reverberated into the ground, into my horse, my saddle, my bloodstream. Even then, I knew this was the pinnacle ride of my ranching career.

Two hours later, horses and cowboys arrived safely at Mud Lake. Each got their graduation certificate—a meadow of beautiful green grass for the horses and a pat on the back and a ham sandwich for the cowboys.

During the four years the wild horses remained at Mustang Meadows, they never stopped trusting us. We moved them and gathered them as easily as you'd push a fork into a slice of peach pie. Each time I rode with the horses, I thrilled at having those mustangs galloping behind me, thundering through the thick grass and reminding me why I took a chance and did something that had never been done before, and did it well, much to my delight and the delight of fifteen hundred wild horses.

PART 3

ON COMMON SENSE

Never kick a cow chip on a hot day.

CHAPTER 11

HOBBLED

We were rounding up one day at Big Pasture, where we had been assembling cattle for a month for our big fall sale. I was nine years old and had long had my eye on the day when I'd become a grown-up cowboy and a good one at that. I was the youngest on the roundup, but I was determined to keep up.

Temps hovered around freezing and it felt mighty cold. The cowboys all wore their winter coats and gloves. This was the day to cut the cattle that we planned to sell and select the replacement heifers that would birth future calves. Being the youngest, I was assigned the job of holding the cut. It's an easy job at the beginning of the day because only a few cows have been cut, but as the day wears on, more and more cows are added to the group so the job becomes more difficult. I would be riding the perimeter of the group to make sure none of the cows wandered off. My sister, Ann, was on the roundup that day too. That meant if a cowboy needed to use the bathroom, he'd ride over a hill out of sight, dismount, and pee.

I was taking my job very seriously. The cold was beginning to creep through my unlined gloves—no cowboy would be caught dead wearing lined gloves—and pretty soon I began to feel the call of Nature. I didn't have anyone to take over my job so I waited. And waited. And waited. When I was about to burst, I rode over the hill, got off my horse, and tried to unbutton my Levi's. My hands were so cold that I couldn't get the buttons undone. I tried and tried, but I had waited too long. I let go. Warm pee ran down my legs and into my boots. I was mortified. Cowboys don't pee on themselves. It just doesn't happen. I started to cry.

I got back on my horse and galloped the mile back to headquarters. I jumped off and ran up to the house. I had to tell my mother what happened. She comforted me and said not to worry about it. I found a clean pair of Levi's and undershorts and warmed up enough so that I could do the buttons. Then she gave me her boots to wear.

My horse and I galloped back to my post. Some of the cows had started wandering off. I had to scurry around to gather them, but I got them back into the herd. Still, I was as embarrassed as a young cowboy could possibly be.

Years later, when I had become the grown-up cowboy I aspired to be, I made sure all my winter gloves were lined. The cowboys gave me a hard time about those gloves. Cowboys take pride in some strange things, but I much preferred warm hands and a little ribbing to soggy boots. By then, of course, I knew not to wait so long to answer Nature's call.

That wasn't the only time I was hobbled by my own actions. I was about to start eighth grade when I read a magazine story about some boys who went camping with their dads. My dad was not about to go camping. Many times, I heard him say that years before he had slept on the ground for his last time. I knew better than to ask him to take me camping, normally a rite of passage for a young man and his father.

I decided every boy should camp out in the wild, so I suggested to my buddy William Kipp that we go on a camping trip. William's father was an alcoholic and wasn't any closer to taking William camping than DA was to taking me. One day, MO went to town to pick up the mail and picked up William, too. I had horses all ready to go and our route mapped out in my mind. We would head to Cottonwood Canyon on the New Mexico part of the ranch where the Gila River ran. It was about twelve miles from headquarters—eight to the highway, then another four to the canyon. It was so remote, you either had to hike in by foot or ride a horse. It was an area where we didn't want our cattle to go because it was too hard to get them out. Big rock bluffs soared a couple of hundred feet above the riverbed. There was a dry waterfall that only ran after a rainstorm. The bluffs and caves had all kinds of Indian pictographs of men and snakes and antelope and suns, most likely from the Hohokams and Apaches. Our plan was to camp, explore, and be adventurers in the wild.

What I didn't know about camping was a lot more than what I did know. I tried to think of everything we would need.

Food and lots of it. Grain for the horses. Sleeping bags and frying pan. Ropes for rappelling. A box of matches. A shovel. It was June, so we didn't have to worry about rain. We'd sleep under the stars on our saddle blankets. I tied all our gear and provisions onto our horses, front and back, since we didn't have packsaddles. By the time William and I set off, we looked pretty hardscrabble.

We arrived late afternoon. I worried our horses would leave and find their way home, so as soon as we dismounted and unloaded, I hobbled them. I dug two water holes in the sand—one for William and me and one for the horses. From previous hikes into the area, I knew this was the only place on the ranch where you could scrape the surface and quickly hit water. Next, we gathered wood and made a fire, thinking we'd better start cooking before we ran out of light. We ended up cooking all the bacon we brought and ate every bit of it. I saved the bacon grease to cook the eggs in the next morning. Before we went to bed, I checked on the horses. I was still worried about them leaving, so I tightened the hobbles again.

William and I stretched out on our saddle blankets and scared each other with ghost stories. It was hard to sleep on the sand. At some point in the middle of the night, I woke up. My first thought was of the horses. I went to check on them, and just to make sure they stayed put, I tightened the hobbles.

We woke up with the sun, of course. The first thing I did was make sure the horses hadn't strayed. When I saw them, I could have wilted. I never felt as sorry for anything I had ever done, or as sorry for an animal, as I did for them. The hobbles had eaten into their legs. Their forelegs were so swollen that I hardly could see the rope. I felt horrible. They hadn't moved one foot. Why had I been so paranoid? If we went riding into the headquarters, somebody was sure to whip my butt. I certainly deserved it. I looked around for first aid. All I had was the bacon grease. I grabbed it, undid the hobbles, and rubbed the grease into their wounds. They weren't crippled for walking, but I'm sure it was uncomfortable. What a big oops.

Thank goodness we had another day of camping. I found some nice grass, moved the horses, and treated them to some grain. They weren't acting like they wanted to get away. Instead of hobbling them, I put a rope around their necks and tied it to a tree. They looked much more comfortable. William and I spent the day exploring the Indian cliff dwellings.

The next day we loaded our gear, less all the food we had eaten, fed the horses again, and rode back to the ranch. When we arrived, no cowboys were around. I got some salve from the barn and rubbed it on the horses' ankles, then turned them out into the pasture. I held my breath for the next few days. Neither horse got infected. I could always see the scars where the hairs had turned white, but no one ever commented on them.

I later took a number of horseback trips into the Gila wilderness and learned the trails pretty well. I was the guide and senior camper on most of those trips. I never told anyone where I learned my skills or why I thought it best not to hobble horses in remote areas. The best part was having the opportunity to give my son, Alan Jr., some pretty fun camping experiences while he was growing up.

CHAPTER 12

COME HELL
OR HIGH WATER

Alan Jr. played high school varsity basketball. One year, Duncan had a pretty good team and managed to qualify for state finals in Chandler, a Phoenix suburb. I had made it a priority to attend every game during the season and certainly wasn't going to miss the state tournament.

The day before Al's first game, my wife Barbara, daughter Marina, and I flew up to Phoenix's Sky Harbor Airport. During the past few days, it had been raining statewide, but we managed to fly out and land between storms. I parked the Cessna at the executive airport, then rented a car at a nearby Budget office. Our plan was to stay with Sandra and her husband John that night, then drive to Al's game the next day.

We arrived at the O'Connor residence in a downpour. It poured all night and into the morning. The rains extended into the White Mountains north of the city, where they melted the snowpack and sent it roaring down the Salt River all the way into Phoenix. During the night, those wild waters had washed away the bridges of some major arteries. According to the morning television news reporter, one bridge remained open. It was the one we needed to cross in order to get to Chandler and Al's afternoon game. We made sure to leave the house early enough to give ourselves extra travel time.

I drove the car back the way we had come the previous day; I planned to get on the freeway near the airport. I turned on the car radio. Every ten minutes, the announcer reminded us how slow traffic was moving. Slow was an understatement. At one point, I heard him say it could take up to four hours to get across town. At that rate, we were on schedule to miss the game. Come hell or high water, I was not going to miss that game. There had to be a different way to get there.

Darn right there was. I had an airplane.

We finally crept as far as the Budget office. I turned into the parking lot, turned in the car, and we started walking the couple of blocks to the executive airport. We could fly across the river, land at the Chandler airport, and take a taxi to the game. Or so I thought. What I didn't know was that the Salt River had run with such force that it had washed out part of the south runway, forcing air traffic control to run all planes from the north runway.

We got in the Cessna and I started it up. I could see at least twenty commercial jets lined up on the one available runway waiting to take off. 737s. 747s. Not one small plane. I was the only fool out there. I called ground control.

"Don't get in any hurry," I was told. "We're using the runway for the big boys so it's going to be a while before we call you. Pull off to the side, and we'll get to you when we can."

I pulled off and we sat for a good thirty minutes. The line never shrank. Tip off loomed closer and closer. Okay, I thought, time to go to Plan C. I started the plane, taxied out, and slid in between a United 707 and a Southwest 737. The pilots were so high that they remained hidden from sight. I felt like a fly on a horse's back. I radioed the tower. "Six Nine Tango ready to go in sequence."

The controller was furious. "Nobody gave you taxi instructions."

"Well, I'm here in line," I said.

He huffed. "All right. You'll depart in sequence. Be aware of wake turbulence, so get out of our airspace as fast as you can." He managed to be very professional and very disapproving at the same time. I was only too happy to get out of his airspace.

We took off and flew across the river, about twelve hundred feet above ground. I knew there was a private airpark outside of Chandler, a couple of miles from the basketball arena. I located the airstrip and made the landing. We were barely out of the plane when a resident pilot happened by and asked what I was doing in this private airpark that didn't cater to stray planes. I said we were trying to get to a basketball game, and I'd pay him to drive us there. He became very accommodating and said sure thing, he'd do that. We arrived in time for the tip-off and watched the entire game. The team won and advanced to the finals, which they didn't win. Nonetheless, it was all very exciting. The high water had come and I caught some hell, but it didn't matter. I got to see my son play.

CHAPTER 13

THE DUDE

I occasionally attended a party hosted by Sandra and John at their Phoenix home. At one of these parties, a friend of John's, whom he had recruited as a lawyer for their firm, came up to me and said, "You're the brother who's the rancher, right?"

After I acknowledged I was, this fellow said, "I was raised in Connecticut, but I'm out here now." As I soon learned, Steve had graduated with honors from Harvard Law School and eagerly accepted John's offer. Steve loved the West and all things western. He wanted to play cowboy, but knew less than nothing about ranching. "I want you to invite me to Lazy B," he said.

"No," I said, reciprocating his directness. I explained that sometimes Sandra would send a dude to the ranch, and it was always a big chore to babysit the dude and keep him out of trouble. I didn't need any more dudes. He wasn't insulted by my refusal.

The next time I attended an O'Connor party, maybe six months later, Steve was there. Again he asked me to invite him to the ranch.

"No," I said. "Having somebody like you along is like having two good men gone."

My comment didn't deter him, because the third time I saw him, he repeated his request. I admired his persistence. After the fourth party we found ourselves attending, I finally said okay, he could come over and ride on the roundup for a couple of days. Steve was smart enough to ask what he could bring to win favor with the cowboys. "About four cases of beer would do it," I said.

On the appointed day, Steve arrived with four ice-cold cases of beer and made an instant friend of all the cowboys. He also brought his horse.

"Has your horse ever been out in deep rocks?" I asked. "Tomorrow we'll be rounding up on the rockiest part of the ranch."

"I don't know. I've only had him in the arena."

"Then you'd better ride one of our horses. They've been raised in rocks since day one. Your horse needs to understands the rocks."

"Nah, that's okay," said Steve. "It'll be good for this old horse to be out there in the rocks, and besides, I want to ride him."

"Bad mistake, but if you insist," I said.

The first day out, we rounded up at Tank 2, a dirt reservoir surrounded by several eight-hundred-foot-high solid rock mountains with cattle scattered from top to bottom. Steve and I rode up the canyon as far as we could go.

"You take the right side, I'll take the left," I said. "We want to scour for cows, top to bottom, and push them down into the canyon."

"Okay," he said. We split up.

I knew he would have a hard time, so I made sure to take the side with more cattle. I kept an eye on him while rounding up my bunches. He had ridden two-thirds up the mountain and was heading toward his first bunch of cows when he arrived at a large area where there had been a rockslide. The loose rocks had no soil to anchor them. If it had been me, I would have ridden above or below it, not across it, but not Steve the Dude. He had his horse start walking right across those loose rocks. When the horse got to the middle, he froze up with fear. Even from the other side of the canyon, I could see the sweat and foam pouring off him. Steve kicked and spurred and shouted at him but the horse wouldn't move. Steve got off and tried to lead him, but the horse still wouldn't move. Steve then got behind him and tried to drive him, but the horse wouldn't budge. Chuckling, I continued gathering my cattle. His horse remained in that one spot for at least a half an hour. Finally, Steve picked up rocks and started throwing them at his horse. The rock throwing dislodged other rocks. I could hear them rolling down the hill. The horse came unglued and started lunging forward. By the time he ended up across the slide on solid ground, all the cattle had turned and gone off the mountain to get away from the ruckus.

Steve got back on his horse and made his way to the bottom of the canyon where I was waiting for him. He didn't know I had seen the whole show. As he rode up, I said, "Well, Steve, how'd it go? Did you gather all the cattle off that hill?"

"I don't know, but if there are any left, I'll buy them right now and take range delivery because I'm not about to climb back up there and run them off."

I broke out laughing. He never offered to bring his own horse out to the ranch again, and for the next twenty years rode whatever horse I provided.

Some years later, Steve returned for another round up. We had just rounded up at Tank 5 and were driving the cattle back to Lost Lake. Steve was in the back of the herd bringing up the drag, and I was in the lead turning the cattle. I still kept a close watch on him. I could see he had his rope down and was roping at the heels of cows to keep them going. A really big bull was the slowest of all the cattle and had to be urged forward. Without warning, Steve roped this bull around the neck. Why he would choose to rope that bull around the neck, I don't know. The bull was bigger than the horse he was riding. I was furious. I was prepared to take out my pocketknife and go cut the rope before that bull got crazy mad. If that happened, there would be no way for Steve to get the rope off its neck.

The bull walked about ten more steps and boom! He fell over. He didn't move. I knew he was dead. Steve hadn't even tightened the rope yet. I had never seen a bull walk along in a herd and drop dead. Nor would I ever see it again. I turned my horse and headed over to the commotion, or lack thereof. The cowboys had all gathered around. There was Steve, a sheepish look on his face, the rope in his hand, and a dead bull at the feet of his horse.

"Steve, why'd you kill my bull?

Steve couldn't answer, he was so flabbergasted.

"What the hell were you thinking roping a grown bull around the neck? That's as dumb an action as I've ever seen cowboying. How the hell did you plan to get that rope off his neck?" I was ninety-nine percent certain he hadn't been the cause of the bull's death, but I wasn't going to let him off the hook that easily. "You're not going to like the bill I'll send you for the price of that bull."

We later determined that the bull had eaten a weed called golden eye. It was spring and golden eye was blooming all over the ranch. If a cow or bull grazes golden eye and then exerts itself, the golden eye can kill it. The golden-eye had saved Steve. The story caused much cowboy gossip back at the ranch and later at the bar. Our Harvard bull-killing dude had made cowboy lore.

CHAPTER 14

THE BIG BURNS

It was early autumn on Lazy B. A crew of cowboys and I were headed out to the Summit corrals, about eight miles from headquarters. The day before, we separated mama cows and their calves and loaded the calves on trucks so they could be delivered to a buyer. This particular morning, we were returning to the corrals to drive the cows back to headquarters first, then on to nearby grazing pastures.

We arrived at the group of distraught mothers just as the sun peeked over the mountains. Mournful bawls filled the air, drowning out the chatter of doves and quail. Of course, no one could tell the mamas that by now their babies were at least five hundred miles away. We had quite a job to get all the heartbroken animals away from the corral, they were so intent to stay there and cry. But after a lot of hard work, we got the cows headed in the right direction and began the slow trek back to headquarters.

The air grew crisper by the minute, and the grieving animals soon stirred up a shroud of dust. We had travelled about four miles when I noticed a large plume of smoke rising from the exact point of headquarters. Jim Brister was in the lead and came riding back to the drag.

"Whadya think, Al?"

"Can't be good," I said. We went through the litany of what could be burning. The main house. The bunkhouse. One of the windmills with a wooden tower. At the moment, there was nothing anyone could do about it. We were too far away. If one of the cowboys galloped in to try and fight the fire, the cows would turn and start heading back to Summit. Besides, what could one cowboy do? So we kept pushing forward, hoping and praying that the families we left there, including my five-year-old son Alan Jr. and his four-year-old cousin Jay, were safe.

For the next ninety minutes, we watched the plume grow darker and wider. Fortunately, the wind never kicked up above a breeze. At last, crew and cows crested the hill overlooking headquarters. Thank goodness no building was on fire. But flames leapt from what earlier in the morning had been two hundred fifty tons of alfalfa hay that I had spent most of the summer hauling to the ranch. It was a year's supply of feed for the horses, milk cows, and weaning calves. The pile had shrunk to my height, and the barn covering the hay had turned into smoldering cinders. I felt like one of those bawling cows.

Alan Jr. and Jay were the first to come running up. Even at age four, Jay was pretty quick on his feet.

"Big Al! Big Al!" he cried. "The good news is we're okay. The bad news is that we were playing with matches and started the hay on fire." He looked at me with big, expectant eyes. How could I holler at a four-year-old telling the truth? I scooped up a boy in each arm and gave them a hard hug.

We ended up buying more hay and cutting back on its use for the rest of the year. Considering the buildings that could have burned, it wasn't a huge disaster, just a medium-sized disaster. When disaster strikes, you do what you need to do to handle it, and then move on. It was a lesson I put to use years later on the South Dakota ranch.

I had just bought Mustang Meadows and didn't have any cattle or horses on it yet. It was summer, and my small crew and I were starting to make improvements. It was a hot, cloudless day when our neighbor, John Hippin, drove through one of our pastures to get to his adjacent pasture. His truck backfired and ignited a grassfire. Instead of getting out to fight it, he took off.

Prairie grassfires can be devastating if left unchecked. The fortunate thing in that part of the world is all the ranchers in the area cooperate every time there's a fire. If they see a plume of smoke, they drop what they're doing, get their equipment, and race to the fire.

Our equipment consisted of a fire truck that the neighboring town of Kilgore had worn out and given to us when they bought their new truck. When I moved in, I made sure to have it serviced and filled with water so it was ready to roll. When we saw that dark smoke, we ran to the truck and raced four miles over the hills, the siren blasting to make the lizards and prairie dogs scramble out of the way.

Neighbors arrived about the same time—some with shovels, some with willing bodies, one with a water tank in the back of his pickup. A large area of pasture was already blackened. A prairie fire can go a hundred yards in two minutes. The strong winds blowing at us didn't help. There were about eight of us, and we had to fight like hell. For a bit there, things teetered on who would win—the fire or us. We eventually contained the fire after it burned about thirty acres.

A year later, a big grass fire started west of us and scorched one hundred thousand acres of good grassland. Fire trucks from a hundred miles away came in to fight that one. They emptied their tanks and had to go refill I don't how many times. Those were some long, hot hours for those firefighters.

My foreman happened to go into a bar not too long after our fire. Who was there but Hippin, and what was he talking about but how his truck started a fire that burned a bunch of prairie grass. Hippin never explained why he didn't get out of his truck, and my foreman never confronted him. It didn't seem worth fighting over, especially since the fire had been put out and the grass would get around to growing soon enough. But Hippin, I'm telling you now, if you're still up there, alive and well, you owe us one.

CHAPTER 15

ALMOST FAMOUS

I was carrying groceries from my Suburban to the doublewide trailer I lived in on Mustang Meadows Ranch. The wild turkeys marched past me, headed toward the ranch road as if setting out on a summer vacation. One of these days I'll follow them, I thought. Maybe I'll learn something. Right then I needed to answer the phone ringing inside.

"Hello," I said. The screen door slammed right as the person said his name. "Sorry, didn't hear you,"

"This is Kevin Costner calling." There was a pause. "Are you the person to speak to about the wild horse sanctuary?"

"Yes, I am. I'm Alan Day."

"If you have a moment, Mr. Day, I'd like to talk to you about your sanctuary. I'm working on a project involving a lot of horses and you might be of help."

I didn't know anyone named Kevin Costner, but said fine, I'd be happy to listen. He proceeded to explain that he was an actor and was directing a movie set in South Dakota. It had to do with Indians and would be filmed on the prairie. He asked a ream of questions about the location of the ranch and its layout, then peppered me with questions about the horses.

"Can you control your horses enough to be able to film them?" he asked.

"You betcha," I said and babbled about how we had trained the horses and could move them in one herd from pasture to pasture. "They're most cooperative," I said, ever the proud parent.

Costner said, "Several of the scenes involve an Indian camp and a river and a large group of horses that will be used as their remuda."

"Well, we have the Little White River that runs through five miles of the ranch," I said.

"I'd like to send you a copy of my script and have you read it," said Costner. "See if you can envision the movie being shot on your ranch."

I agreed and we hung up. I walked back outside. The turkeys were fat-rumped specks waddling up the last hill of the road before it turned out of sight. A funny feeling settled over me. That had been a strange conversation. I never went to movies. What if this guy wasn't an actor? What if I was being flimflammed by a hustler? I went back inside and called my buddy Mike Berry in Tucson, the biggest movie buff I knew.

"You ever heard of an actor by the name of Kevin Coogan?" I asked him.

"Kevin Coogan? No, never heard of him."

"Well, some guy named Kevin Coogan just called me and insinuated he's some big movie star and is looking to shoot a film up here on the ranch. I'm wondering if he's for real or giving me a line."

"Kevin Coogan, huh? You sure that's his name?" asked Mike.

"Well, yeah. I'm pretty sure," I said, not feeling so sure. Names and I have never gotten along well. I heard a creak like a chair leaning back, and then a hollow slap, like a hand hitting something.

"You wouldn't by chance mean Kevin Costner?"

"Uh, yeah. I might mean Kevin Costner." So I misplaced a few letters. Mike assured me he was the real deal and advised me to rent *Field of Dreams* and *Silverado*. I told him I'd have to get a VCR first.

A few days later, Fed Ex delivered a box to the ranch. I settled in at my desk, took my pocketknife, slit the end of the box, and slid out a slim black binder filled with a little over a hundred pages of paper. I flipped it open to the first page. *Dances with Wolves* written by Michael Blake. Every free moment that weekend, I picked up the screenplay. By Sunday night, I had finished it. Even with its foreign notations and directions, the story gripped me. I never read a script and didn't have anything to compare it to, but I could envision it being shot on Mustang Meadows Ranch, especially the scenes of an Indian camp on the banks of a river with a horse herd nearby. Costner called mid-week and I shared my thoughts.

"If you don't mind, I'd like to come see your ranch and the horses," he said.

"Works with me," I said.

Two weeks later, I landed my 182 Cessna at the Front Range Airport in Denver and went into the pilot's lounge where Costner and I had arranged to meet. He was bringing his producer Jim Wilson with him. About ten people were seated at tables. Two guys in jeans and cowboy boots sat at one. They were about the same age, both with sandy brown hair and athletic. I wasn't sure who was Costner and who was Wilson, so I introduced myself.

Costner sat next to me in the plane and Wilson took the back seat. Costner mentioned that he had never flown in such a small airplane. We taxied out to the run up area. I picked up my well-used checklist from the dash. I had it memorized, but didn't want to appear too nonchalant about piloting, so went down the list with my finger, checking the steering wheel for free action, cycled the prop, checked oil pressure, checked the mags. Costner leaned around the seat and said to Wilson, "This guy has to read the instruction manual before taking off." Great, I had a comedian and actor on board.

During the seventy-five minute flight, Costner told me more about his vision for the movie. It would be his first effort directing. He felt fully confident that he could do it, but Hollywood questioned his ability and refused to put up the money. Eventually, he found funding from an investor in Italy. I well knew the language of naysayers. It has a limited vocabulary of words like "never," "can't" and "crazy," phrases like "no way," "what's he thinking" and the ultimate wet blanket, "it's impossible." If I had taken the cynics' advice to heart, I might own a ranch in South Dakota, but the only horses on it would be a half-dozen saddle horses. Paddling upstream seemed to be my role in life, and Costner seemed to be sharing the same canoe.

We landed in Valentine, Nebraska and hopped in the Suburban. An hour later, I turned the truck off the state road and drove under the sign for Mustang Meadows Ranch. The sun sat like a ripe peach over the horizon and the hills glowed yellow, as if showing off for Hollywood. "This is how I envisioned it," Costner said. "This light is perfect."

I pulled up to my doublewide trailer. "Guys, we'll have to wait to see the horses and the ranch until tomorrow," I said. "How about if I grill some steaks and we have a little dinner?"

"Suits us just fine," said Kevin. They grabbed their duffel bags, and I showed them where they would be staying in the doublewide.

We ate steaks and made a dent in a fifth of scotch. Kevin shared his background and his struggle getting into the movie business. He had an easygoing, affable manner about him.

The next day was perfect. A brisk breeze, but not enough to dislodge a hat. The greens of early summer. A warm sun. The three of us set out in the Suburban to explore the ranch. Costner asked many questions. How far was it to hotels and restaurants? Where were the biggest hills on the ranch? Where was the little White River?

"It's just over the next hill," I said.

He said, "Good, then let's park here. I want to see the view as we crest the hill on foot."

At the top of the hill, we stopped. He explained this was the scene the cameras would reveal. He framed his hands into a lens and put it up to his eye. "Perfect," I thought I heard him whisper. We spent the rest of the morning in the area. Would he have to get permission to film from anyone but me? No, I owned the property. Could he build a camp here? Yes, no problem. How wide was the river? Do you think these trees work in the background? He was gathering information and making serious decisions. I knew the drill.

The ranch seemed to be calling to him. The location, however, was not. Most of the filming is done in the early morning and late afternoon when the light is best. Having a crew stay at a hotel two hours from the shoot would require everyone to get up at about three AM to start doing makeup, load gear, eat breakfast, then drive. That's early even for a cowboy.

It was mid-afternoon when we pulled into the cemetery pasture, named for the Indian burial mounds on it. I stopped the Suburban on a hilltop. Down below, fifteen hundred mustangs grazed. They had become accustomed to the Suburban by now and didn't pay us much attention. A pheasant cock was far less amused by our presence. The bird started running around one of the mounds squawking. It must have amused Costner, because he got out of the car and started chasing it and doing the funky chicken dance. Maybe he had concentrated so hard by the Little White that he needed an outlet. Jim and I sat in the truck while Costner and the pheasant cock ran around. The wind was blowing in the direction of the horses and carried their noisy conversation right into the sensitive ears of the mustangs.

A few horses started pawing the ground. Their heads alert, their tails swishing, they began to vibrate like a hive of irritated bees. Costner and the bird kept up their antics. A few of the horses started to run, a signal to the others to pay attention and get moving. Within a minute, the herd was stampeding. Jim and I got out of the truck to watch.

"Kevin, look what you've done," yelled Jim.

Costner stopped and looked at the horses. "Oh man," he said. "What happened to them?"

The herd circled the entire pasture, then slowed down once they didn't hear any more grating noise. I wished that I had a camera to capture the scene.

The next day, I flew the boys up to Pierre to meet with a fellow who owned a herd of buffalo. By then, Costner knew he loved the land, the river, the horses, but he was discouraged about the logistics. He said that he would let me know if they would be using the ranch. He was a man with a job to do and was taking that job seriously and throwing himself into it. If my ranch fit into that job, then so be it; if not, that was okay too. He said he would love to come back and do some horseback riding and hunting on the ranch. I told him the door was always open.

A few weeks later, Costner called. He had found a site about fifteen miles outside of Rapid City, South Dakota. It would be better for the crew, but he appreciated being able to see Mustang Meadows Ranch. Sure was a gorgeous place. I wished him luck on his project.

In the end, I was glad that the movie wasn't shot on the ranch. A lot of wheels and feet would have trampled the sandy soil in a small area. Surely, the grass would have been damaged and who knows what else. I had been concerned about that, but reasoned the land would recover. The movie's incredible popularity resulted in curious people visiting the site where it had been shot. They came at all hours of the day and all days. The trampling of their feet and ruts left by their vehicles would have seriously damaged the fragile vegetation and created blowouts, giant potholes formed by high winds. I would be to blame. I figured it was better just to enjoy the movie on the silver screen, with its scenes of beautiful rolling prairie.

PART 4

ON LISTENING

Never miss a good chance to shut up.

CHAPTER 16

CLOUD SEEDING

I was sitting in my office in late July enduring one of the harshest, ugliest droughts we had ever experienced on Lazy B. Not one drop of rain had fallen during the past nine months. Since the grass hadn't greened up with protein, we had to haul feed to keep the cows from starving to death. I was wondering what I had done wrong to cause God to punish me. Out of frustration, I picked up the phone and called my sister, Sandra, who at the time was serving as the majority leader in the state senate. Sandra answered the phone.

"Do you know how dry it is here on the ranch?" I said.

"Yes," she said, "it's that dry all over Arizona. Getting close to a crisis."

"Well, why don't you do something about it?" I said, only half joking. Sandra was one of the world's best problem solvers.

95

She said, "What do you want me to do?"

Out of nowhere popped an idea. "How about starting a cloud seeding program to make it rain?"

"My goodness," said Sandra. "Now that's a thought. Let me see what I can do."

I hung up feeling better at having dumped my load of angst onto her shoulders. I didn't give our conversation another thought.

About a week later, Sandra called back. After checking around various places in Washington D.C., she was directed to the Office of Emergency Preparedness. She spoke to a General Lincoln, the head of the office, who was quite responsive to my suggestion. He asked if it were dry on the Indian reservations. Sandra said yes, very dry. He told her that if she could get the Indian tribal leaders to request federal assistance with cloud seeding, the federal coffers would open and at least money would rain down on Arizona. Sandra immediately called Peter McDonald, the chairman of the Navajo Nation and asked him if he would like to get some rain made. He said absolutely, yes. A contract was issued and Safford, Arizona, a town forty-five miles west of Lazy B, became cloud seeding central. I was overwhelmed with the response. It was incredible. You make a phone call, bitch a little bit to your sister, and boom! Life changes. Or so you think.

If the government could seed above the reservations, I was pretty certain they could seed above the rest of the state. I jumped into my Cessna and flew over to the Safford airport to check things out. Three airplanes were parked in a row. I could see the silver iodide flares mounted under the wings, pointing backward like small missiles. Silver iodide helps make rain by acting as a nucleating agent. When silver iodide molecules make their way into clouds, water molecules attach to them, and when heavy enough, they fall out of the clouds as rain.

It didn't take long to locate the crews lounging in the hangar doing what pilots do, talking flying and drinking coffee. They were happy to greet a new face and only too happy to tell me that they were professional cloud seeders and were there on a government contract. "But you can't make rain out of blue sky," one said. They were hoping for moisture and clouds to invade the area within the next week.

I said, "When that happens, my ranch is due east. Can you make sure to fly over it and let loose your magic flares?"

Much to my surprise, they quickly turned me down. Their contract with the government called for them to fly only in Arizona and no closer than thirty miles to any of the state's borders. That meant they would miss Lazy B entirely. I argued and begged for them to make an exception. It's federal money, I pointed out, and reminded them that I was the one who had inspired their contract. They were kind and patient to this impatient cowboy, but firm in their position. I asked why some knucklehead bureaucrat in Washington had drawn up the contract that way. They suggested I call my senator and ask. I went home frustrated, but determined.

The next day, I returned to refresh the argument. They again turned me down. I again was undeterred. By the third day, they had about enough of me.

One of the pilots said, "Why don't you seed the clouds yourself? That's your 182, right?"

I nodded.

"All you need to do is make a removable bracket and bolt it onto the landing gear," he said. "We can tell you where to get the flares and how to use them."

My mind exploded with possibility. I was so desperate for rain. "Spell it out and don't miss a detail," I said.

Per their suggestions, I ordered the flares from Olin Mathieson Chemical in St. Louis, Missouri and bought a car battery. I built a bracket in my shop, then bolted it onto my plane's landing gear. The flares soon arrived. After I secured them in the bracket, I threaded the two lead wires from each flare through the door and into the cockpit where I had stored the car battery. In order to fire the flares, I would need to touch the wires to the battery's terminals. I would do this while the plane circled at the base of a targeted cloud. The flare would burn for eight minutes and release its silver iodide crystals. The cloud's updraft would suck up the silver iodide. The pilots had instructed me to seed cumulus clouds with a minimum updraft of five hundred feet per minute. The seeded clouds might rain, they might not. Seeding a cloud that was about to rain could double or triple the amount of rainfall.

By the time I was ready to seed, moisture had moved into Arizona and cumulus clouds were forming. I soon discovered that flying at 12,500 feet at the base of a big cumulus cloud was not your everyday flying experience. It was turbulent to the extreme. Sometimes it felt like I was riding a bucking horse. I always strapped myself in with a shoulder harness, but I had to unstrap it to climb in the backseat to fire the flares. The plane would buck so much it would throw me all over the cockpit. I became frightened that I might hit my head and get knocked out.

I flew eight minutes under a cloud candidate, and when the flare stopped burning, I scouted out another cloud. The bracket held six flares so I could seed six clouds. Quite often a thunderstorm would start within minutes of seeding a cloud. On a number of occasions, when I descended from the base of a cloud to the ranch, which took about sixteen minutes, two inches of water already would be covering the runway, all from the rain I had just initiated. I would be laughing and screaming and cheering as I hydroplaned to a stop. I tried seeding all types of clouds and pretty quickly learned which clouds were ripe and which weren't ready. If I seeded one that wasn't ready, in about four minutes it would disappear. Poof, gone. I started feeling godlike.

One time, I approached a very large cloud with a very dark bottom. As I flew under it, I hit a huge updraft. My gauge indicated it was a 3,000-foot-a-minute updraft. Within seconds, I was sucked up into the middle of the cloud, a place I really didn't want to be. Total fog. Rain. No sense of direction. It might have been cold, but I was sweating so much, I wouldn't have known. I had no idea where I was going. I tried to keep my cool, pointed the nose down, and started to power dive. The airspeed indicator quickly jumped to the red line. If I exceeded that line, I was in danger of shaking off a wing, especially in turbulence, and believe me, I was in heavy-duty turbulence. I kept thinking, kiss your ass goodbye, cowboy. Fortunately, the power dive brought me out of the bottom of that cloud. I never bothered to tell my wife or family about my near miss.

Twice, I invited people to accompany me. One was my foreman Cole, who flew with me quite a little, and the other was a friend. Both of them had the exact same reaction when we landed. "That was an exhilarating ride, Al. But if you need somebody to go with you next time, please don't call me."

Every morning, I worked on the ranch and watched the clouds develop. I planned my day so that I was available for seeding in the afternoon when the clouds typically rained. My work became vastly easier because green grass began sprouting everywhere. The cows had smiles on their faces. They were putting on weight and all of our reservoirs were full of water. In fact, rain was greening the entire area, not just Lazy B. At the end of the season, our records showed a fifty percent greater-than-normal rainfall. I will always believe that my seeding caused at least some of that increase, if not all.

I went into the fall with a great feeling of success and happiness and ordered another case of flares for the next summer. Cumulus clouds only appeared during the monsoon season, not during winter. I was afraid to tell anyone about my venture because I didn't know how many rules and laws I was breaking by being a wildcat seeder. Plus, I figured people would be funny with their reactions. Some people might say I washed out their reservoir; others might say I stole the rain that would have come to their ranch. I didn't want to face such accusations. So I kept my success to myself.

The following summer, I was ready to seed well before summer rains that usually began around the first of July and extended through September. I seeded all summer with spectacular success. The danger was no different. Flying at

12,500 feet gave me a headache every time. For whatever reason, I never brought oxygen or a helmet, even though I was still getting bounced around in the cockpit. After landing, I would have to lie down for two hours. By the first of October, rainfall on the ranch was seventy percent above normal. What an amazing summer it was. I felt as if I had created a new dimension to Arizona ranching and assumed that was a good thing.

Then one day at the beginning of October, clouds appeared sooner than usual. I watched with glee as they seemed to grow and multiply before my eyes. It was getting to look like the best day I'd ever seen for possible rains. I drove up early to the hangar and had just opened the pickup door to get out and go to the plane when a voice spoke to me. "Don't fly today," it said.

I looked around, trying to determine where the voice came from. I didn't think anyone was within two miles of my hangar.

The voice repeated: "Don't fly today."

I was dumbfounded. In all my life, I had never heard a voice without a body speak to me. It repeated itself again. Was I hearing the voice through my ears or hearing it through my mind? I couldn't determine. It repeated the same words at least six more times.

I started arguing with it out loud. "But this looks like the best day ever to seed," I said.

"Don't fly today," it said.

I began to feel quite troubled. Should I pay attention to this or not? I rationalized with myself. We've had a fabulous summer already. The tanks are full. The grass is green. The cows are fat. We're approaching fall with the ranch in the best shape it has ever been. Maybe I don't really need to seed. I shut the pickup door and drove back to the headquarters.

That afternoon, it rained so hard that the Gila River flooded, and the flood was so severe that it washed part of the town of Duncan away, including the elementary school. Three people drowned and the area suffered multi-million-dollar damage. I had a very strong reaction to all of those events. My main reaction was thank you, God, for looking after me and persuading me not to fly. I'll always believe that if I'd flown, the flood might have been worse, and more people might have died. I would have carried that guilt to my grave.

I never seeded again. It became clear that I had been playing God, and I didn't really know what I was doing. I'm not particularly religious, but some force had my back and had been kind to me.

When I sold the ranch, I still had half a case of flares. I didn't tell the buyers what they were for. I have no idea if they remain there, but I'm pretty certain they'll never be used. And that's just fine by me.

CHAPTER 17

TWISTER AND
THE PRICKLY PEAR

Twister caught my eye when he was quite young. A combination of red, blue, and dun roan, he was a handsome horse with a nicely shaped head and a pleasant attitude. One of the Lazy B cowboys named him Twister. At the time, I didn't know why. When we went to break him, Twister proved to be gentle and displayed an eagerness to work cattle, so I chose him for my string. The problem was that I didn't have the time to train him to be the extraordinary cutting horse I thought he could be. I did, however, know a trainer who could possibly put a shine on Twister's emerging ability. Terri agreed to help, so I loaded Twister in the trailer and dropped him off for some advanced schooling with his new teacher.

About four months later, Terri called. "I think it's time for you to come get your horse," she said. When I arrived, she gave me the full report.

"He's a good solid horse, a fine ride, and he sure does act like he wants to cut cattle. But Al, I just don't think he has that innate sense of knowing when to move to make the cut. I tried again and again to get him in the right place. If I didn't deliberately spur him and point him at the exact cow to be cut, it wasn't going to happen."

A good cutting horse knows exactly where to go and when to move without being told. Twister couldn't figure out those two essentials. So much for calling this one right.

"It doesn't mean he's a failure," said Terri. "You know as well as I do he'll make a fine ranch horse."

I petted Twister's nose and told him it was okay. He had given it a good try. He hung his head a little sheepishly, but gave me a quick nuzzle. I decided he could stay in my string. I'd start him off with easy days and figure out what he could and couldn't handle.

I chose to ride Twister the day Miles Brown visited Lazy B. Miles, the Bureau of Land Management range conservationist for our ranch, had a college degree but lacked hands-on experience. I had taken it upon myself during the past months to let Miles see some things and have some experiences he might not otherwise have had. I suggested we load our horses in the trailer and drive the hour out to Horseshoe Mountain. I wanted to check the grass and natural water catchment on top of one of the mesas. If the recent monsoon had filled the catchment with sufficient water, I would drive thirty head of heifers up there for the winter. Twister was still young, no more than four years old, but since Terri had ridden him quite a little, he could probably handle the trek up the two-thousand-foot rise.

We arrived at our destination and saddled up. I took the lead along the narrow trail hugging the side of the mountain. Autumn was just beginning to make itself known, and the day wanted to be enjoyed, so we assumed an easy pace. The mountain wall rose steeply above us on the left and fell off just as steeply on the right. It looked to be about a hundred and fifty feet down to the rocky canyon floor. About halfway up, Twister decided to take a breather, not unusual for a horse, especially a young one climbing a steep grade. He stopped, and I let him catch his breath. Then, out of the blue, he did a maneuver I had never seen a horse do. He began backing down the trail. I lightly spurred him. Instead of stepping forward, Twister's legs began to collapse and he started to sink. Uh oh, I thought, something's gone wrong. Best I get off this downward moving elevator. Just as I started to swing out of the saddle on the uphill side of the trail, Twister started to tilt toward the downhill side. Before I had time to dismount, Twister fell over, taking me with him. The next thing I knew, I was fifteen feet downhill, still partially in the saddle and beginning to roll. Less than a second later, I was spread-eagled right in the middle of a very large prickly pear cactus. Before I could say ouch, Twister rolled over me, his nine hundred pounds mashing my entire backside into the spiny cactus pads. This was not a sensation I wanted to be schooled in. I heard him tumble away. Then all went quiet.

"Al, holy Jesus. Are you hurt?"

I looked up at Miles looking down at me. "Hell, yes, I'm hurt," I said. "I'm just not sure in how many ways." I could feel cactus spines through my jeans.

Miles edged down the mountainside and extended a hand. The little needles in my palm reminded me I should have been wearing gloves. I moved my legs and arms. My hips and pelvis, previously injured in an airplane wreck, already hurt but they seemed intact. I was half afraid to look for Twister. Fortunately, he was standing upright in the canyon, saddle in place. I took a step. Every muscle felt like it had tiny pins in it.

Miles went another ten feet down and retrieved my hat. "What do we do now?" he said, handing it to me.

I settled it on my head to the tune of a thousand needles moving inside me. "Gotta gather my wits about me for a moment. This is a helluva wreck."

Miles started pulling clumps of cactus off me. After ten minutes, at my suggestion, he picked his way down to the bottom of the canyon to collect Twister. The canyon was studded with such huge boulders that they had to find an alternative trail. Meanwhile, I went uphill to fetch Miles' horse. No way could a human pincushion sit in a saddle. We limped our way the mile back down the mountain. Each step seemed to take ten minutes. After what felt like forever, we made it to the truck. Miles and Twister were waiting for us.

Miles loaded the horses in the trailer and helped me into the back of the pickup, where I stood during the return ride to headquarters. My wife spent over two hours plucking out spines that she could see and a little less time chewing on me for getting in such a predicament. Since predicaments weren't anything new, she gave up after awhile and plucked in silence. The tiniest of thorns finally worked themselves out after six weeks. It was a grin-and-bear-it time for riding horses and moving in general.

Twister never became my favorite horse, and I'm sure I never became his favorite rider. Maybe he had tried to tell me something as we walked up that mountain, and I failed to hear him. If so, I wish he had spoken a little louder. As it was, it took a thousand prickers to get my attention. Some lessons in life are just more painful than others. Best to learn those quickly and not have to repeat the course.

CHAPTER 18

CANDY

I had been managing Lazy B full-time for about eight years and had just lost a horse from my string, so I needed a replacement. I spent some time observing our crop of young horses and chose a good-looking filly whose mama I had ridden years before. She had been a nice horse, very solid and good to ride. Like her mother, this filly was blond, with broad shoulders, a large frame, and an amiable disposition, all traits of a good horse. I decided to name her Candy after one of our family's friends, whose sunny disposition and pretty face always made me smile.

Our longtime cowboy, Claude Tippets, heard me calling the newest horse in our remuda Candy. He said, "Alan, that's a really bad name for that horse."

"What makes you say that?" I said. "Didn't know a bad name made a bad horse."

"It's too pretty a name. That filly can't carry a name like that and carry you at the same time. She'll die."

Maybe Claude was losing it. Next he'd be telling me to keep salt in my chaps to throw over my shoulder. I shrugged. "Well, we'll see about that."

"Nope, she won't live. Ya named her wrong," he insisted. "She should be called Squaw Piss."

If I had seen a crystal ball sitting on the corral post maybe I would have changed her name, even to Squaw Piss, but I didn't, so she remained Candy, and Candy remained sweet with one exception. When I went to fetch her in the horse pasture, she'd nuzzle me and enjoy being petted. She remained cheerful while being saddled, but as soon as I'd get on her, she'd put her head down and go to bucking. She couldn't buck very hard, so she never bucked me off, but when the cycle started, I had a hard time getting her to stop. I figured she was one of those young horses that had to go through the bucking phase. Eventually I'd just ride her out of it, so I kept riding her in an effort to do that.

She still hadn't ditched her habit the day I saddled her for a pleasure ride. The summer rains had spit-shined the ranch and persuaded grass to grow, especially in the big floodwater draw that ran past headquarters in the east pasture. An inviting blanket of green covered its normally dry dirt bottom. About a mile and a half down, the draw spread out into a big hole, maybe a hundred yards long and fifty yards wide, which remained bone dry until the summer rains filled it. Then it turned into a twelve-foot-deep water hole. I thought we'd go check it out, then ride through the pasture.

We hadn't even left the corral when Candy went to bucking. When I got on her she bucked. When we went out the gates she bucked. When we rode through the draw she bucked. Each time, she'd buck a few jumps, and I'd get her pulled up and scold her either verbally or with a little bit of corporal punishment—a spur, a slap of the reins—enough to let her know she was misbehaving. This went on and on as we progressed down the draw. I thought she'd get her head up and start paying attention to the work we were doing, which was nothing more than me riding her trying to enjoy the scenery. But no. She had to buck.

By the time we arrived at the water hole, we were hot and downright irritated with each other. The waterline had edged up as far as it could go without spilling onto the land. The calm water invited us to cool our tempers and wash the sweat off. I decided we would go for a swim. Since a horse can't buck in water, at least that nonsense would end for a bit. I rode Candy to the edge of the water, but she refused to put her feet in. I spurred her. She turned left. I turned her back and spurred her again. She turned right. That darn horse was doing everything possible to avoid the water. This was ridiculous. I grabbed the get-down rope with its big cotton knot at the end, swung it with one hand and popped her a good one on the hip.

I should have named her Pegasus because Candy just about sprouted wings. She leapt into the air and plunged into the middle of the water. I slid off the saddle still holding the reins, prepared to do what cowboys do when you swim with a horse. With one hand, you either hold the saddle horn or the tail and let the horse pull you around. Kind of a western version of swimming with a dolphin, though I wouldn't exactly call twenty-pound chaps and a pair of pointed leather boots a version of a wetsuit.

I didn't get a chance to grab the saddle horn or Candy's tail. Her back end sank, her front legs began to flail, and her head thrashed. She couldn't swim! I had never seen a horse that couldn't swim. I tightened my grip on the reins and tried to keep her head above water. One leg came down on my head and knocked me under water. I kicked back up. A hoof hit my shoulder hard, another glanced my ear. I dodged another hit, still trying to hold her head up. Water was getting in her nose, and she was snorting and rolling her body back and forth and trying to climb all over me. I went under again, this time with a mouthful of water. I came up gasping for air. The water roiled around us. Candy pawed harder, desperate to find solid ground. She was starting to push me around and under. I couldn't hold her up anymore. I could barely hold myself up. I let go of the reins.

By the time my boots hit bottom, the muddy water had swallowed Candy. No burping bubbles marred its dark surface. I crawled up onto dry land, my chest heaving with exhaustion. What felt like a twenty-minute struggle surely had been no more than five minutes. Hell, maybe three minutes. I was numb to the bruises I sustained, numb to the glory that had been in the day. Disaster had struck with the fury of a cyclone, a tidal wave, a horse that couldn't swim. How could a horse not swim? They were like dogs. Every dog can swim. Candy had tried to tell me she couldn't swim, but in my frustration and need to win the battle, I had failed to listen. I was not numb to the feeling of being a fool and to having my heart broken by my own stubbornness.

I sloshed the mile and a half back to headquarters in a flabbergasted fog. I could still see our trail through the grass. I had been out for a ride on a young, healthy, pretty horse and now she was dead. I stumbled my way over uneven ground, wet chaps swishing, boots sloshing, talking out loud trying to figure out the whole situation. If I had named her Squaw Piss would she have died? Probably. But I couldn't say for sure. All I knew was that I had failed her. And here I was doing the cowboy walk of shame back to the ranch, my horse on the bottom of a stinking water hole. I was an idiot. I lost a horse and a friend. What kind of a cowboy was I?

That day I was a jumble of recriminations – guilt, anger, regret. I was not in a place to learn. But in the following weeks and months, I looked hard at my role in Candy's death and acknowledged that I had failed my horse by not paying attention. I vowed from that point on to listen and be receptive to what my horses were telling me.

CHAPTER 19

HUNG UP

The son of the boss sometimes gets to thinking he's bigger than he should be, and once in a while needs to be taken down a notch or two. I was no exception.

We had a cowboy, Gene Johnson, who worked for us for a while along with three of his brothers. Gene had a lot of good common sense. He didn't need a cocky six-year-old to start telling him what to do, but one day I did just that.

"I'm not doing that," said Gene.

I said, "You better do it or I'll tell my dad and he'll fire you."

Gene wasn't a bit intimidated. "If you don't shut up, I'll hang you by your belt loop on the bunkhouse hook, and I'll drive off and leave you hanging."

"You wouldn't dare," said sassy kid.

Gene did dare. He picked me up, walked over to the bunkhouse, lifted the water bag off the big hook, and hung me up instead. I kicked and screamed who-knows-what as he drove off. When my belt loop finally broke and I dropped to the ground, I thought about going to DA and telling him what had happened, but my good sense told me I better not. I better just keep quiet about things. My dad probably would have said, "Gene should have hung you up even more securely."

Years later I was hung up again, but in a different way. I was still cocky, but not very sassy. I was a student at the University of Arizona heading home to the ranch for Christmas vacation. Freeways hadn't been built yet, so I was driving the two-lane highway that went through downtown Benson, a town about forty-five miles east of Tucson. The local policeman in Benson had the identical car to mine except that mine was souped-up a bit. It was a '57 Chevy, dark blue. I had bought it back in high school and done a little work on it. Every time I saw that Benson police car, I would smirk and think I could outrun him.

It was a sleepy Sunday morning when I hit downtown Benson and saw the police car parked beside the road. Without even thinking, I hit second gear and burned a strip of rubber right in front of that cop. It was an outright invitation to chase me. I was pretty sure that I could outrun him. It worked. Here he came. I went screaming through the east side of Benson, under the railroad tracks and up the other side. I was doing over a hundred when who should appear beside the road but a state trooper. The state police at that time drove a souped-up Oldsmobile, a car much faster than my car. The trooper caught me in a flash and wrote me up for reckless driving. He said, "You have to go back and face the judge right now."

I had no choice, Sunday or not. I followed the state trooper back to Benson. The judge's office was in his home, so I waited in the driveway for him to get out of church. He was a nice man and asked me to explain what the hell I had been doing driving over one hundred miles per hour through Benson on a Sunday morning. I owned up to doing it and didn't offer an excuse.

"The fine's a hundred and twenty dollars," he said.

"I don't have that much money, sir."

He looked at my driver's license. "Are you from Duncan?"

"Yes, sir," I said

"What do you do in Duncan?"

I said I lived on a ranch.

"Will you be working over Christmas?"

"Yes, sir," I replied. "Every day."

"Will you hold on to your earnings and bring me the money on your way back to school?

I said, "Yes, sir. Thank you, sir."

A month later, I stopped back at the judge's home and handed him the money. From that point on, I kept that old Chevy under one hundred miles per hour. As far as I know, the judge never told anyone my story. And neither did I.

CHAPTER 20

THE VOICE OF AUTHORITY

When I started working on Lazy B after college, I quickly learned that my dad expected me to step up to the manager level. What I didn't anticipate was his reluctance to give me one ounce of his authority or power. Anything new I tried to do on the ranch, he severely criticized. He was what we now call a control freak. He disapproved of all newer grazing systems and modern equipment. He made do with pump engines installed in 1915. He was especially proud of his nice herd of Hereford cows and would show them off to anyone visiting the ranch.

The Herefords were pretty cattle imported to the U.S. from Great Britain before the turn of the century. They thrived in the lush English pastures, but when they arrived in the harsh southwestern desert, they were not happy inhabitants. The light pigment around their eyes made them subject to eye cancer, which many of them contracted, and their shorter legs and thinner hooves were not compatible with Arizona's hot, sandy soil.

As a hands-on manager intent on bringing fresh ideas to the ranch, I suggested we buy some different breeds of cattle and try them in the desert. My father strenuously objected. When I said we only would buy two Charolais and two Brahman bulls, he realized the resulting crossbred calves wouldn't overwhelm his Hereford, so he went to grumbling instead of squawking. The crossbreeding experiment resulted in heavier calves, but we ended up having problems with some of the bulls. I changed tactics. I recently had been introduced to cattle specifically bred for the Arizona desert called Barzona, a solid red, long-legged, hardy breed. When I brought the first group of Barzona to the ranch, DA said, "You're going the wrong way. Everybody knows the best cattle are Hereford." After several years, it was evident the calves and mothers thrived in the desert.

When I started buying more Barzona bulls to breed with our Hereford cows, my father's objections grew stronger and more frequent. It was tough pushing ahead against his wishes. "The Herefords are better mothers," he'd say. "They give more milk. The calves will sell better in the market being pure Hereford. You know my Herefords are better cattle."

I could show him that Barzona calves outweighed the Hereford calves by more than one hundred pounds at weaning time. I could show him that Barzona cows would breed annually at a rate of ninety-two percent. The Herefords bred at seventy-five percent. The Hereford cow was worn out and ready for the slaughter plant by age ten, and many times by age nine. The Barzonas lasted until twelve or thirteen years and were productive the entire time. Yet DA would end every one of our arguments with, "You know my Herefords are better cattle."

His opposition became so fierce that he started writing letters to Sandra and Ann. *Alan is driving us to bankruptcy with these damn cattle,* he wrote more than once.

Sandra finally called. "Alan, are we really facing bankruptcy?"

I said, "Sandra, let me have enough rope to hang myself. If I'm truly doing bad, it will come falling down around my ears."

Sandra was loyal to DA, but she soon learned he was crying wolf because every year our profit grew. Gradually DA recognized that his letters weren't sounding any alarms and Sandra and Ann concluded DA was being DA. I had been his target throughout my life, right up there with FDR, the BLM, and the governor. The cowboys would do something wrong, and I would get criticized for it. It's twice as difficult doing something you think is right when every step is unsupported. But after years of climbing the steep mountain, you eventually reach the top.

About ten years into breeding Barzona cattle, I decided one summer to keep a group of calves through the winter rather than selling them in the fall. It turned out to be a lovely winter followed by a green spring so the calves grew rapidly. These Barzona calves were particularly fat and perky.

On the first day of our spring roundup, I gathered about a hundred head of the calves. The cowboys and I had driven them into one of the corrals at headquarters. It was late afternoon, and

I was walking across a corral to catch a horse that I needed to shoe for the following day. Out of nowhere, a voice spoke. It was loud and clear. "Show your father these cattle," it said. I only had heard a voice like this once before. Still, it was so strange that it stopped me in my tracks. "Show your father these cattle," it said again. "I'm too busy, " I said out loud. "I have to get ready for tomorrow."

The voice repeated itself. "Show your father these cattle."

This time, I knew to pay attention, so I quieted the inner debate. I went back to the barn, told the cowboys I had something to do and for them to go up to the bunkhouse and have a cup of coffee. I didn't explain what it was I had to do because I didn't want to see the look of disbelief on their faces. I then went up to the big house. My father was up and feeling good that day. He didn't get out around the ranch any more because he had emphysema, probably due to smoking too many cigarettes, and he stayed connected to his oxygen tank. But that afternoon, he had his mask off.

I said, "DA, I gathered some really pretty calves today. Would you like to come see them?" He had noticed all the dust and commotion down in the corral, but hadn't been able to see the calves.

"Why, that'd be right nice," he said. I helped him into his car and drove him down to the corral. He couldn't walk far, so I drove the car into the corral. I used it to push the herd into one corner of the corral, then shifted into park and let them walk out past the car.

"Look at how big that steer is," said DA, pointing. "Look how pretty that one is. How much will that big one weigh?"

When they all had filtered out of the corner, he said, "Drive 'em up into the other corner and let them come out again. "

We spent almost an hour in the corral looking at those pretty steers. On the way back to the house, he turned to me and said, "Alan, that's the finest set of steers ever raised at Lazy B ranch."

I was overwhelmed. He had never said one positive thing about the Barzona cattle. But here he was, not automatically defaulting to his statement about Hereford being better. I knew this was as close as he could come to apologizing for all of his rude remarks through the years. I shared his joy in how handsome those steers were.

About seven the next morning, I was out in the middle of a pasture starting to round up another section of the ranch when I saw a pickup speeding out toward us. I knew it wasn't one of our cowboys because we were all horseback. I went galloping toward the truck to find out what the problem was. Small problems don't detract from roundups, only cataclysmic events do. I shoved the thought of what it might be to the back of my mind. Glenda Moore, the wife of a cowboy who worked for us, sat behind the wheel looking disheveled and pale. I knew before she spoke what had happened.

"Your dad died in his sleep last night," she said.

Even though a part of me expected her to say that, I was shocked. He had been so good yesterday. Though incredibly sad, as the next few days progressed I was overwhelmed with gratitude for the hour DA and I had shared. It wasn't a coincidence that I had shown him the cattle. It was a reconciliation of decades of conflict. Without that voice speaking up, it wouldn't have happened. What if I hadn't listened? I would still be living with anger, regret and who knows what else. But, as it was, sharing one simple moment erased a lifetime of conflict and hurt.

PART 5

ON PERSISTENCE

If Plan A doesn't work, stay calm.
The alphabet has 25 more letters.

CHAPTER 21

ALL IN A DAY'S WORK

It was the first day of summer vacation. I had just returned to the ranch, having finished my junior year of high school. Claude Tippets, one of our cowboys, must have noticed I was up for grabs. "Let's you and me head over to Z-Bar-L," he said after breakfast. "There's a corral fence needs replacing." I said, fine, if that's what needs doing, let's go do it.

We loaded digging equipment, a five-gallon Igloo water jug, and lunch into the pickup and drove east about ten miles to Z-Bar-L, an old homestead that Lazy B had acquired years after the place had been abandoned. A well had been drilled there about 1915, and a windmill and corrals built around the same time. The old house had been broken up board-by-board and used in branding and cooking fires. The big round corral fence was still standing, but the middle cross-fence was falling down. All of the fence posts, most likely originals, had rotted. We spent part of the first day hauling the old posts out of the way and lining up railroad ties that we would use for the new fence. Then we got busy digging post holes.

We each had a shovel, and between the two of us, one heavy digging crow bar. The bar was called Big George. That's the name it always had. It was so big and heavy that if you used Big George all day, you were a man. Big George had a digging point on the end of it. What we discovered on the first hole was that after digging with our shovels through eight inches or so of sandy soil, we hit caliche, a sedimentary rock that rivals concrete in hardness. Out came Big George.

When we banged Big George into the caliche, we broke off tiny pieces of the rock, about a quarter inch thick and the size of a fifty-cent piece. After fifteen or twenty minutes with Big George, I'd be used up. While Claude took his turn with BG, I'd get down on my hands and knees and with a tomato soup can, scoop out the flakes I had just loosened until the bottom of the hole was clean. I'd gulp some water and be ready to go at it again. Except for a quick lunch, we worked that way all day. Banging, sweating, scooping, drinking. It wasn't a race to see who could work faster. It was just steady, hot, hard work. At the end of the eight-hour day, each of us had dug a three-foot deep hole and drunk our half of the five gallons of water. We packed up the pickup and headed home.

The next day we were at it again. Banging, sweating, scooping, drinking, and sweating some more. The midday temp had to be at least a hundred degrees. By four o'clock we were out of water so we packed up. The next day we brought the Igloo and a canvas water bag. Once again, by the end of the day, we each had dug another post hole. I had a feeling Claude was satisfied with the work. Never had he said, "Golly, this is hard" or "Wish we could go faster." He just kept working strong and steady.

Being a teen and impatient, at the end of the week I finally said, "Claude, isn't there a better or faster way to dig these holes?"

Claude's answer to me was as valuable as a whole semester in school. "Well, what we're doin' here is good honest work," he said, leaning on Big George and wiping the sweat off his forehead. "We'll finish when we finish. And when we finish this job, there'll be another job that needs doing. So let's not look ahead. Let's work at doin' the best job we can right here. That way we can rest assured that these posts will still be standing up when we're dead and gone."

Standing there drenched in sweat with blistered hands, I realized that I had just learned exactly who Claude Tippets was. How could I have anything but respect for this man who day after day got himself out on the ranch doing honest hard work that brought him complete satisfaction? I accepted Claude's simple and direct analysis. From that point on, I never resented having to spend each day banging on rock-hard caliche with Big George. But that didn't mean I couldn't keep an eye out for better post-hole-digging technology.

Several years after that summer with Claude, we had to build a whole new set of corrals at Antelope Well. It involved maybe ten times as many post holes as we had dug at Z-Bar-L. Harold Bishop, the local concrete guy in Lordsburg, had just bought a backhoe. It was the first one around, the first one any of us had seen. I went to Harold and asked if his backhoe had a twelve-inch-wide digging bucket because that was the size of our fencepost holes. Yes, he said. I then asked if that backhoe had enough hydraulic pressure to dig through caliche. Sure does, he said.

I went to Antelope Well, marked each post hole, then hired Harold and his backhoe. He dug all of those holes in one day. Progress in spades. A few years after that, I bought a backhoe for Lazy B. Besides Big George, it was one of the most useful tools on the ranch.

When Claude got old and retired, I'd go visit him at his little house in Duncan. One day he said in his gruff voice, "Come in here boy, I have something I wanna give you." We went into his house and he handed me his spurs that he had used on the roundup for fifty years. "I don't think I'll need these any more," he said.

It was such a touching moment neither of us could speak. We could only cry. To this day, I've never gotten an acknowledgment in my life that was better than that. His spurs still hang on the wall next to my front door.

I always felt like I learned a huge lesson from Claude about doing the best job possible. Claude never required attention, never asked for help, saw jobs on the ranch that needed doing and went and did them. He was grudging with his approval and rarely complimented anyone. Still, in ranch school, if there is such a thing, Claude was the teacher I never forgot and the one who handed me my diploma: a pair of spurs. Whenever I see those spurs, I'm reminded to do the best

I can at whatever I'm doing that particular day. When I do it, I always have a sense that somewhere above Claude is looking down at me with approval.

CHAPTER 22

ROPING THE BULL

hen are you gonna come get your bull? He's tramplin' our cotton plants and almost lives in our alfalfa." Charlie Clouse didn't sound angry, just a little frustrated.

"I'd be happy to," I said into the phone, "but what are you talking about, Charlie?" Charlie owned a farm down on the Gila River across from Lazy B.

"One of your bulls has been jumping the fence," he said.

This was news to me. Apparently, for the past year, this bull would hightail it over the fence and maraud through the fields, crushing cotton plants, feasting on alfalfa and making a general mess of things. Charlie would run him into the thickets by the river where he hid until Charlie disappeared. Then the naughty guy would jump the fence again, and the cycle would repeat.

"Why didn't you tell me about this sooner? I would have come and gotten him." I felt a prickle of irritation. I knew Charlie had a lousy fence that he didn't maintain. I could already tell this bull had taught himself well. He had the upper hand and was working the system. Now we'd have to retrain him, if that were even possible.

"Will you rope him if you have to?" asked Charlie. "Because that's one big sucker of a bull."

"Yeah, Charlie, if I need to rope him, I will." I didn't particularly want to rope a full-grown bull, but if that were the only way to gather him, I would do it. Shooting him wasn't an option.

"Then tell me when you're gonna do it cuz I'll stay home from work. I want to see this one."

Oh good grief. What were we running, a rodeo? "Stay home tomorrow, Charlie, and we'll come get that bull."

If Saber had been in my string, I would have chosen him for the job, but this was the pre-Saber era, so the next morning I went out and caught Tequila, a young mare with mousy, grulla coloring that I was riding at the time. She was Candy's older sister, but from the start was a sweet, kind gal. She had a big solid frame and strong shoulders, and she never shied away from work. She liked to work cattle, but wasn't a topnotch cow horse or particularly athletic. We had never been in a situation together that demanded she give everything, so I didn't know her limits. Since she was the biggest horse in my string, I chose her for the job, hoping she could handle it. I recruited Cole Webb, our foreman, and Vince Sanchez, a Lazy B cowboy, to accompany me. Cole's horse was smaller than Tequila, but I didn't think that would pose a problem. Vince would work the corral gate on foot. We saddled the horses, loaded them in the trailer, drove over to the Clouse farm and parked near an old corral adjacent to the cotton field. The plan was to run the bull in there, then load him into the trailer.

The corral was cluttered with wood and debris and had loose rub boards hanging down. I assigned Vince clean-up duty. Cole and I headed our horses out along the levy that separated the Gila River from Charlie's fields. A barbed wire fence ran the length of the levy. The ground on both sides of the fence was a mosaic of giant hoof prints. We opened a gate to get to the river where we thought the bull might be hanging out and left it open so we could backtrack through it. The ground had long since gulped the monsoon rains so the slender river barely filled one-eighth of its quarter-mile bed. Thickets of scrub brush and mesquite grew in the sand, perfect hideouts for a crafty animal not quite crafty enough to hide his trail. We followed a fresh track of prints that led straight to a thicket.

There was a muted drum roll of thudding hooves, a splash of water and a big red bull with a massive set of horns jumped out front and center about eighty yards ahead of us. Except for the tips having been cut off the horns years before, he could have been the poster bull for Merrill Lynch. He must have weighed eighteen hundred pounds. He glared at us defiantly, then bolted into the next thicket. He might have been all hulk, but he was quicker than a NFL running back.

Cole and I loped toward him, hoping to haze him out of the thicket. Instead he raced downstream to the next clump of brush. We approached and he dashed across the river and ducked behind more mesquite and tamarisk. This tacking back and forth across the Gila, with him getting the better of us, quickly grew tiresome. I decided to call a different play. I hand signaled to Cole that I was going to slip around to the far side of the brush where the bull would exit. Cole knew the play. He stayed on the opposite side and started making a racket. The bull burst out. He looked startled to see me twenty yards away. The lid popped off the action box.

Tequila charged the bull. I threw my rope, intending to rope him around the neck so I could choke him if I had to. A bull can't fight if he can't breathe. But instead, the rope pulled up around his horns. I dallied up. Tequila jammed her front legs straight out. The bull turned and headed off, dragging her twelve hundred pounds like a sled in a southwestern Iditarod. A hundred yards later he stopped to catch his breath. Cole rode up on the side of him and hazed him toward the corral. For the next twenty minutes, the fight spread over the river valley. When the bull turned toward the corral, we gave him slack and followed him. Then he tired, stopped, and turned back toward us. Not what you want: a feisty bull facing you. Cole fought him until he turned toward the corral, and once again, we made progress. I felt Tequila beginning to tire. I was sorry that I had roped this sucker; it was more than Tequila could handle, but she wasn't going to quit. She remained brave and stayed with the job.

"Come on, girl. I can see the corral." The bull jerked the rope, and I let him pull us. "Cole, you take the rope," I yelled. It seemed like a good time to give Tequila a break. I loosened the taut rope, threw Cole the slack, and he dallied on his saddle horn. The bull must have felt the rope's tension change, because as soon as Cole dallied up that big old lug took off, practically pulling Cole's horse on her nose. Her nine hundred pounds were no match for his brute strength. I could see this was a mistake.

The bull climbed up the levee and veered through the open gate. Tequila and I galloped up next to Cole and reclaimed the rope. Tequila gave it her all. She grunted, tightened her shoulders, leaned back and locked her legs. The bull slowed, but didn't stop. He was furious that he was still roped and in a fix. He hunched forward and stomped down the levee toward the cotton field. Out of the corner of my eye, I noticed a red dirt bike at the edge of the field. I could see two teenagers in a row of cotton, hoeing weeds. They must have arrived while we were chasing the bull in the riverbed.

The bull caught site of the cycle and made a beeline for it. Tequila lost her leverage and galloped behind him. That ornery beast made for the bike as if it were a matador's red cape. One of the boys stood up and pointed. "Hey, that's our bike," he hollered. "Leave it alone." They started running toward it.

"Get away! I can't control him," I yelled, motioning them to turn back. I could feel the bull's strength and determination pulling the rope. All I could do was hang on and pray he was more interested in the bike than the boys.

The bull never paused. He ran right up to that motorcycle, hooked his horns under it and tossed it in the air like it was a play toy. Everything halted—the boys, the bull, Tequila, Cole—except the bike. We watched that two-wheeler fly twenty feet in the air, then plummet toward earth. It landed with a metal-crunching thud. The boys took off running in the opposite direction. Shit. They probably saved up a year's salary of cotton hoeing money to buy that motorcycle. Now there it lay, crumpled to death.

The bull shook his head, snorted and stomped a few times. Tequila raised her head. She wasn't going to let him get the last laugh if she could help it. He looked around as if contemplating what additional damage he could do. He charged forward, jerking Tequila. She followed for a few steps, then splayed her feet and leaned back as hard as she could. I could feel her shoulders shake.

"Hang in there, girl," I said. "Maybe he'll head for the corral."

Her quivering muscles told me her shoulders were sore and she was having a hard time holding the bull. She couldn't dig in enough, and we had to give slack when he pulled. Desperation hovered around the scene. If I let the bull go, he could turn and charge Cole or me or run after the boys. None of us wanted to see an angry, horned, one-ton animal barreling toward him. I heard a motor sputtering behind me. I turned in the saddle enough to see Charlie Clouse coming up the levee on his old popping Johnny, a 4020 John Deere tractor with a front-end loader. He must have seen our predicament because he wheeled in through the gate and pulled up beside me.

"Looks like the battle's in full swing," he shouted. "Can I help?"

"Lord, I hope so. We're just about overmatched here." The bull stopped and turned to look at us, deciding whether to go forward or retrace his steps toward us. Charlie accelerated. He steered the tractor in front of Tequila and bumped that old bull none too gently. The bull wheeled around and took off straight toward the corral. Our convoy followed at high speed. Along the edge of the cotton field we went, then the alfalfa field. The bull stopped abruptly and looked back. Charlie was on him with the John Deere, and off the bull ran, not happy about being bumped again. The alfalfa field bordered the corral.

"Tequila, we gotta get him in the corral." She pulled back a little, tightening the rope. The bull pulled to the right in response. If he kept on running, he'd go through the corral gate in less than a minute.

Vince stood at the ready, both hands on the open gate. Cole hazed the bull on one side and Charlie rode the tractor close on the other side. That big old red bull was running straight as an arrow. I unwound the dally and held the rope in my hand. The bull ran through the corral gate. I tossed the rope in behind him, and Vince slammed the gate shut.

The bull stopped in the middle of the small corral. He swung his head in both directions, stomped around in a one-eighty and went to snorting and pawing. He was one pissed off dude at having lost the battle.

"Tequila, you get the purple heart," I said patting her shoulder. I was so proud of the way she hung in there to the very end. If I had known it was going to be such a huge chore, I wouldn't have subjected her to it. Every once in a while I bit off more than I could chew, and this was one of those times. I dismounted and let the reins drop. She wasn't going anywhere. She was exhausted, sore and used up. My heart went out to her. "You'll get extra grain tonight, sweetheart, after we get this bad boy home." I rubbed on her neck and nose.

Charlie, Cole, Vince and I spent the next quarter hour trying to get the bull up the loading chute into the trailer. We swung long sticks in front of him, yelled, did everything we could think of. If we had a red cape, we would have stood at the top of the chute and waved it. But that gol' darn animal stood his ground, flames jumping out of his eyes, looking for something to vent his fury on. When our frustration began to top out, Vince volunteered to do the insane.

"I'll run across the corral," he said, like he had done it before a dozen times. "He's going to charge me. But just before I get to the chute, I'll jump for the fence. The bull will run under me and up the chute. Problem solved." He shrugged his shoulders like it was no big deal. .

Vince was fast and young, but this was Mr. Macho he was talking about, stud of the bull kingdom. I said, "You sure you want to do that? I've seen this guy run and you can be damn sure he'll give you a chase."

Vince eyed his competitor. He gave another casual cowboy shrug that said risking his life was no big deal. "I can do it, Boss. How else are we going to get him up that ramp?"

Standing there in the heat of a stalemate, I couldn't answer his question. "Okay," I said, my glass of confidence half-empty. "But put some fire in those boots."

Vince slipped around to the other side of the corral and climbed over the fence. He hit the ground running and yelling. He ran like a jackrabbit, but that bull's muscles were spring-loaded and ready to snap. He lurched into a run. Vince threw a hand and foot on the fence at the same time the bull hiked his horns under Vince's butt. Vince went flying over the corral fence, head over tail. I winced. He thumped down on his back. The bull surveyed his work and clopped up the wooden chute into the trailer.

Vince didn't move for a few moments. The wind in him had to be knocked from here to Lazy B. Cole hustled to secure the bull in the trailer, and Charlie and I jogged over to Vince prepared to give first aid. Before we got to him, Vince stood up, wobbled a step and said with a grin, "Got that sonofabitch, didn't I?"

"You practicing to be a rodeo clown?" said Charlie, slapping him on the back. I was glad he was in one piece.

Back at Lazy B, we unloaded the bull into his own corral, where he stomped around for the rest of the day.

I led Tequila out of the trailer. She limped her way into the horse corral. "You stay here for a rest, girl. Eat some hay, take it easy." I put a hand on each shoulder and rubbed. I didn't like to see her in pain. "I couldn't be more proud of you, Tequila. You gave me everything you had and never quit even when it got down and dirty." She nosed my shirt.

We left the bull in the corral. Every time I looked his way, he got pissed and made me understand that he was not the forgiving type. He had lost his way of life and wasn't going to enter rehab easily. Every few days, one of the cowboys would load hay in the pickup, drive it into the corral, and get out to throw it in the feed manger. That bull would charge and the cowboy would jump back in the truck. I made a judgment to never turn that animal out again. If we did and went to gather him, he might charge us or catch someone unaware and really do some damage. The following week I loaded him into the trailer and hauled him to the livestock auction. He made a lot of hamburger for someone.

Charlie told me who the kids were that owned the motorcycle. I called them and said if you can't fix your motorcycle, I'll buy you a new one. That's what I ended up doing.

I gave Tequila a week in the corral and fed her extra hay. She walked around with a stiff gait, a sign of strained shoulder muscles. I thought it best to give her a long rest, so I turned her out for six months in the horse pasture, then brought her in, but she was still lame. Her shoulders had not healed right and she walked with a limp. I felt twinges of sadness and regret every time I looked at her. She was still handsome and young, much too good a horse to sell, so I turned her out with the broodmares to raise colts, and she raised some really fine ones.

CHAPTER 23

WITCHES, WELLS, AND WINDMILLS

My dad was the resident well expert on the ranch. He knew more about wells, pumps, and windmills than anybody. When a pump or windmill part had to be repaired, he was Johnny-on-the-spot, tools in hand. He didn't trust anyone else to do the job as well as he could, and he probably was right. One time, DA sent Claude Tippets to start a pump engine at Horse Camp. We desperately needed water in the tank. Claude left at four in the morning. At noon, he still hadn't returned. At three o'clock, DA decided he'd better find out what was gong on. An hour later, he arrived at Horse Camp. There was Claude, still cranking on the balky engine. He had been cranking on it all day. It wasn't in Claude's nature to ever give up.

"What's wrong, Claude?"

"The damn motor won't run."

"Does it have gas?"

"Hell, yes, Harry. Do you think I'm dumb?"

"Does it have spark?"

"Course it has spark."

DA said it should run then. He turned it over once and that balky engine fired and started running. It made Claude so angry that he quit his job right on the spot and stormed off. My dad let him have a day or two to cool down, then went and begged him to come back to work, which Claude did.

The one thing DA did not like to do was climb the windmill towers, nor did any of the other cowboys. They would do it under duress and with protest. For some reason, I wasn't afraid of heights, so I became the tower monkey. When DA slowed down, all maintenance and repair fell on my shoulders. Since water is the life-blood of a ranch, I took the job seriously.

Finding water on Lazy B could be a challenge. Under DA's reign, first there would be talk of drilling. This might last a year or two. Then, after more discussion and what if's, he would choose the location. Next came the drilling. Plenty of dry holes were drilled over the decades. My dad occasionally would hire a dowser, also known as a water witch, to pinpoint the source of the water. For some folks, water witching is right up there with psychic predictions. I didn't necessarily believe in witching wells, but I strongly disliked drilling dry holes. Ralph Johnson, brother of cowboy Gene Johnson, claimed to have the power to find water and had a track record to prove it. No one in our family had the touch. We all tried but to no avail. So when I wanted to dig a well, I called Ralph.

Most dowsers use a forked peach tree branch. They walk along until the tip of the branch nosedives. That's where water should be located. Ralph's technique was to take two welding rods and bend them at ninety degrees into an L-shape. As he walked, he held them with the long part of the rods sticking out in front. When they crossed, he'd say that's where the water is and even say how deep we had to dig to find it. I never understood how he could know the depth, and he never bothered to explain, but he was right more often than wrong. Once some underground pipes sprang a leak. The fiddlefarts who buried them hadn't left the treasure map of where to find them. Again I called in Ralph. He located the pipeline within minutes, even tracked the bends in the pipe. Saved me a boatload of time and money. I hired Ralph at least five times to locate wells. In each case, we found water and at the depth he predicted.

After the wells were drilled and pumps and windmills installed, the upkeep began. One day Cole and I were pulling the sucker rods out of one of our deepest wells. Cole drove the jeep to pull a series of cables that lifted the rods so I could unbuckle each joint. I was unscrewing pieces of sucker rod, one from another. As I struggled with one of the joints, the wrench slipped out of my hand, flipped back, and landed on my middle finger. Laid it straight across the back of my hand. Broken bones punctured the skin. It was plain to see that I had a compound fracture.

Cole suggested we go to the hospital. My first thought was no way. We were really low on water. The cattle needed us to finish the job. We forged ahead and pulled the rest of the rods, put new leathers on the pump, then put all five hundred feet of rods back down in the well. I kept my finger out of the way as best I could.

When we finished, I acknowledged the pain in my finger. Cole insisted we go to the hospital, and this time I agreed. A physician's assistant was on duty. He cleaned up the wound, put the finger back so it pointed in the right direction, and set it in a splint. He asked me if I wanted pain pills.

"I'm in some pain," I said, "but I'd rather not have pills."

"Do you like to drink beer?" he asked.

"Yes, I've been known to drink beer."

"Find yourself a bar and drink three or four beers," he said.

Cole and I set out to pick up the prescription. We knew exactly where to stop. The Threeway Bar between Duncan and Clifton. When I went into the bar to follow the doctor's orders, my hand was hurting something awful. I asked the bartender if she had a baggie, and she did, so I asked her to fill it with ice. I stuck my hand in the baggie, rubber-banded it around my wrist, and started drinking beer with my other hand.

About twenty minutes later, the bartender said, "I'm gonna have to ask you to leave." I was mystified. She said, "You've run several of my customers off."

"How the hell did I do that?"

"Look down at your hand."

The bag of ice had turned cherry red. The blood had soaked through the bandages. I extended my apologies and Cole and I skedaddled. It was the only time I've gotten kicked out of a bar.

Altogether, we had thirty windmills on the ranch. Over time, we gradually substituted solar pumps for many of the windmills. Almost every day was sunshiny, but only some days did the wind blow; the solar pumps pumped more water than the windmills did. I refused, however, to take down the two windmills at headquarters. They were landmarks, and I took great pride in them. They sat on giant wooden towers, not steel like most of the other towers. Those two were in place by 1915 and still worked beautifully in the 50s, 60s, 70s and 80s. No one else in the area had windmills that big. They were so big you could see them from ten miles away. When I sold the ranch in 1993, they were still able to pump water. When I returned a few years later, one of the windmills was gone. The new owners got so much grief for tearing it down, they went back to the collector who had bought it from them, bought it back, and hired someone to rebuild it. The last time I saw those two windmills, the fan blades were turning, but they weren't connected to the pump underground. You could hear them squeak and squawk as the weight of the pump changed from upstroke to downstroke. I still love those windmills. I visit Lazy B every now and then, and when I see those towers, I always feel like I've come home.

CHAPTER 24

TAILING UP OLD COWS

One of the summer rituals at the ranch during most of my grade school years was tailing up old, thin cows. Ranching in those days was a lot more primitive, and ranchers didn't care for their cattle's health as well as they did in later years when they routinely bought supplemental feed. About every other year, we would have a dry spring and if we'd had no winter moisture, the plants wouldn't green up. Since the nutritional value of the previous year's growth was very low, some of our older cows would get so thin that they would be close to death. If Rastus found them in that state, he would slowly drive them back to the headquarters where we would feed them hay and nutritious feed. Some of these old cows would get so weak that if they lay down, they wouldn't have enough strength to get up again to eat or drink. In that case, a group of three cowboys went morning and evening to tail up the old cows.

Two cowboys would put a rope under the cow's chest, then get on either side of her. The third cowboy, usually the strongest, would get behind the cow and wrap her tail around his neck and hold onto the bush of the tail. They would all crouch down, and on the count of three gave a mighty effort to pick up this six-hundred-pound cow and get her on her feet. The cowboys made fun of the guy at the backend because quite often the tail was covered with poop, and he'd have a brown ring around his neck after he tailed up a bunch of cows. It was not a badge of honor.

If the cow had a will to live, she would stay standing and happily munch on her hay and drink water, her tail still having enough kick to swat flies. Some of the cows lost their will to live and wouldn't put any effort into standing. The cowboys would try again and again to stand them up and get them to support their own weight, but those cows just wanted to stay at ground level. The rule of thumb was that if a cow refused to stand, she would probably die within a short period of time, even a couple of days.

The interesting part was that some of the cows seemed grateful for the help they received in getting up. But at least half the old cows were angry. Once they got standing, they would try to turn around and charge their helpers. When they did, they usually fell back down. So the cowboys would pick them up again and hopefully get them interested in eating the hay and taking a drink so they could quietly and quickly slide away.

How many did we save? Maybe fifty percent. It always was a happy time when an old cow regained her strength, got off the good feed, and didn't need help any more. Often, my dad waited too long to save a cow. A lot of old cows wear their teeth off and then get thin. They should be sold before that happens. "That old cow has made a good mother and might have one more good calf," he would say, when he should've been selling her. She got a reprieve from being sold.

When I was about five, I wanted to be part of the tailing up process. I would take a flake of hay to the cow and put it right in front of her. We'd all feel good if she ate it. The angry cows, though, would charge me, try to butt me and knock me down. It's a frightening thing when you're not much more than knee-high and you see a six-hundred-pound cow with blood in her eyes wanting to trample you. But I was determined to do what the cowboys did.

One of the scariest times I had happened one day when the cowboys tailed up a cow that was getting a lot better and a lot stronger and was almost ready to be released from the hospital pen. She was strong enough to help the cowboys lift her, and as soon as she got on her feet, she charged forward. At that moment, I was walking into the corral with hay in my arms. A double-armful of hay. That cow saw me and here she came, running right at me. I dropped the hay and turned to run, but she was the faster of us. I ran lickety-split, as fast as my five-year-old legs could go. I looked back over my shoulder, and she was about a foot away. I kept running, then put my hand back. Her head was right there. My hand was on her face and she was running and pushing me forward. I could feel her blowing snot on me. I think I ran the fastest I ever ran in my life because I was literally running for my life. I thought the end was near. The cowboys were leaning against the fence yelling, "Run Alan, run!" She finally stopped. I kept running out of pure fright. I was so frightened, I had to leave the corral and sit down and collect my wits. I was glad to escape unharmed.

When I got to managing the ranch, I made it a rule that I would never let a cow become thin enough to have to be tailed up. I tried to grow more grass for the cattle. I tried to cull the cattle more accurately. Fortunately the scene was never repeated. No cattle charged. No cowboys ran. I was glad when that part of history became history. And the badge of honor, well, it made itself known in other ways.

CHAPTER 25

BLONDIE

My partner in the Nebraska ranch, Allan Stratman, unexpectedly showed up one Saturday at Lazy B headquarters pulling a horse trailer behind his pickup. He had driven the three hours from Sonoita, Arizona where he lived. I was in the house and saw him drive up and walked out to greet him. My eight-year-old daughter Sarah, who had been playing nearby, and her dog Boots, joined me.

"Hey, Al. How you doin'? I brought you and Sarah here a little something." Stratman opened the trailer door and backed out a quarter horse palomino mare. She was tall, about fifteen-and-a-half hands, sleek, and beautifully put together, with an intelligent head.

"Meet Blondie," he said, holding the lead rope out to Sarah. "She's about to move in with you."

Sarah looked at me as if I could explain what was happening here. I had no clue so answered with the same quizzical look. Sarah took the rope. "Hey, Blondie." Blondie lifted her head in quick acknowledgment, then turned to check out her surroundings.

Stratman explained that he had bought Blondie six months ago. She came from a lineage of topnotch quarter horses. He had been trying to break her since. "But she's so hard headed I've had next to no luck breaking her," he said. "Yesterday I got to thinking she just might be better off with a female trainer." He put a hand on Sarah's shoulder. "You're the finest young horsewoman I've ever seen, and I think she belongs with you."

Sarah's eyes widened. "Do you want me to train her for you?"

"Nope. She's yours. I give her to you, and I wish you better luck than what I've had with her." Sarah looked as if she had been handed the biggest and best Christmas present from under the tree. Blondie looked down her muzzle at the small, pig-tailed creature bouncing on the tips of her tennies.

With that and a brief visit, Santa Claus drove off into the horizon, a cloud of magical dust in his wake. We stood there awestruck, rubbing on our newest family member. Sarah already had the look of love.

"Go on," I said. "Get your boots. Let's see what this girl has to offer."

Stratman was right. Blondie could be a real butthead. Sarah wanted to train her to be a jumper, because she loved horse jumping and the competition it offered. But that rebel of a mare had her own ideas about how the world works. She'd grab the bit in her teeth and cold jaw, then run off with Sarah, refusing to do what Sarah wanted. More than once, Blondie threw her head up and hit Sarah right in the face and hurt her. But Sarah never cried. In fact, Blondie couldn't do anything to make Sarah fear her or abandon the task of breaking her.

One day I came in from work and saw Sarah on Blondie. I went over to the corral to check on her.

"Dad, when I want her to gallop, she wants to buck. Here, watch." Sarah spurred Blondie and that horse went to bucking across the corral. I couldn't do a thing but watch and be ready to scoop up Sarah if she flew off. Half way across the corral, Sarah looked back at me, grinning. "Look Dad, isn't she cute?" It was one female will against another and Sarah was determined to win.

Another day, I noticed the two of them in the jumping arena.

"How's it going, Sarah?"

"Dad, I can get Blondie to jump the regular jumps with the poles across, but not the roll top." They must have been working at it for a while because she sounded frustrated. The roll top was solid and wide, but only three feet high, the same height as the pole jumps Blondie easily cleared. "Can you help me?"

"Run her at it and show me what she does."

Sarah rode straight at the jump. Blondie stopped right in front of it. The next time, Blondie veered right. Every time Sarah tried to jump her over the roll top, Blondie refused.

I had an idea. I hauled over two corral panels from the shed and set one at either end of the roll top at an angle, creating a V to prevent Blondie from veering. It didn't take that horse but a few runs to figure out that she could turn in front of the panels. If Sarah managed to get her inside the wings, Blondie stopped at the roll top and refused to jump. Sarah tried this and that, all to no avail. The frustration factor was beginning to multiply. Without saying anything to Sarah, I picked up a piece of old plastic pipe lying on the ground and got in position near the jump. Sarah lined up Blondie and started riding her. The second Blondie started to stop, I swatted her a good one right across the hips. Blondie jumped about twenty feet forward, but not over the roll top. Sarah landed behind the saddle but didn't fall off.

"Dad! What are you doing? Don't hurt my horse."

"I'm not hurting her," I said. "I wanted to see if I could change her mind. This is a test of wills. Your will says one thing, and hers says another."

"But that's not the way to do it," said Sarah. She scrambled back in the saddle, adding some further tongue lashes.

We worked with Blondie for a while longer without success. By this time, all of us had lost our temper. Blondie had her head set in every direction but over the jump. Sarah was angry with Blondie but angrier with me, and I was angry with Blondie for being so stubborn. We were locked up in a box of frustration with no productive place to go. I pushed my mind out of the box, breathed in some fresh air and did some thinking. Sarah tried the jump again. Blondie stopped short again.

"Is Squaw in the corral?" I asked. Squaw was Sarah's other horse.

"Yes," said Sarah.

"Go get her. I'll stand here and hold Blondie. When you get back, I want you to take the roll top with Squaw. I'm going to have Blondie watch you jump."

Sarah stuck out her chin. "That's a dumb idea. Blondie's not going to jump just by watching another horse do it."

"Sarah, do you have a better idea? We're all angry and we're up against the wall here. I don't have another idea, but if you have one, now's the time to lay it out. Otherwise go get Squaw and let's try it. I agree it probably won't work, but maybe it will give us time to cool off." Sarah rolled her eyes, dismounted and huffed off to get Squaw.

She returned to the arena, leading Squaw with Boots the dog in tow. Wherever Sarah and Squaw went, Boots went, so Sarah, Squaw and Boots all took the roll top.

"Now turn around and jump it coming the other way."

"This is stupid," Sarah muttered. Yeah, it probably is, I thought, but I didn't admit it out loud.

The threesome prepared to jump. I squeezed Blondie's halter and forced her head in Sarah's direction. "Now you pay attention to this, you hard-headed bitch. Look how Squaw jumps." No response from Blondie.

"Do it again," I said.

Sarah, Squaw and Boots jumped four more times each way. I kept a tight grip on Blondie and told her each time to pay attention. She quietly stood her ground.

"Let's try Blondie now." Sarah rode Squaw over and swapped lead ropes with me. "Boots, stay here," I said.

The three of us watched as Sarah and Blondie readied and started toward the jump. When Blondie came to the roll top, she shifted her weight onto her back legs and pushed off the ground. She cleared that jump like she had done it a hundred times before. Sarah quickly turned her and jumped her the other direction, just to make sure it wasn't a fluke. She jumped her again and again. Boots and I joined Sarah and Blondie for a little congratulatory hoopla.

The switch had flipped in Blondie, and with the flip came the pledge of allegiance. From that day forward, Blondie acquiesced to Sarah's every bidding—and not just with jumping. Blondie was eager to read Sarah's mind and did just that as often as possible. She and Sarah went on to win so many shows I lost count.

PART 6

ON TRUST

Never trust a man who agrees with you.
He's probably wrong.

CHAPTER 26

A CASE OF BAD GAS

The airplane had become my second pickup. Almost every morning I flew around the ranch to check water levels in the tanks and make sure cattle weren't hung up in corners of pastures, especially if we had just moved them to fresh pasture. The plane also came in handy for the forty-five minute trip to Tucson to attend University of Arizona basketball games.

It was January and the Wildcats were having a good season. My wife Barbara and fourteen-year-old daughter Marina and I had tickets for a weekend game. I went to the hangar to fuel the plane. The day before, I had received a twelve-hundred-gallon delivery from Chevron distributor Rex Kipp, one of my best friends. As fuel glugged into the plane's tank, something seemed off. Usually fuel looks greenish, but this fuel had a different tint than normal. I dribbled some on the wing and watched to see if it beaded up with water, but it didn't. I drained each of the plane's fuel tanks and the carburetor three times, thinking that if there were impurities, they would show up. Whatever drained didn't alarm me. After doing the protocol checks, all appeared normal. Still, something didn't seem right.

The three of us boarded, with Barbara in front and Marina in back. We strapped in, and I taxied to the end of the runway. It was mid-afternoon with a light breeze and the sun still bright in the sky. I went through the take-off checklist—checked the mags, the prop, everything I typically did, and everything seemed normal. I gave the bird power, went into a standard take-off roll, lifted off and started to climb. We had reached about sixty feet when the motor quit. It went completely dead, as if I had turned it off. My mind jumped into emergency mode. Don't turn. Keep the nose down. Land straight ahead. We dropped down past the runway just where a series of gullies two or three feet deep crossed my line of flight. We hit those gullies, and that's the last thing I remember.

When I came to, I was hanging upside down in my seat with blood pooled below me. I popped loose from the seatbelt, dropped down to the ceiling, kicked open the door, and crawled out. I could smell fuel. I suspected it was leaking and was worried the plane would catch on fire. My hips and legs screamed with pain. I couldn't walk, but I managed to crawl back inside the plane and unbuckle Barbara, who was unconscious, and crawl with her outside past the end of the wing. I crawled back, unbuckled Marina, and started to drag her out. She was coming to and helped me some. She was dazed and wasn't sure where she was, but once out of the plane, she stood up and walked.

"Marina," I said, "We crashed the plane. We need help." She looked at me like she had no idea who I was. I said, "Walk back down the runway, get in the car, and drive to the house." It was about a mile away.

Marina was so dazed that I had to repeat the instructions several times before she left. Shortly after, Barbara came to and was able to walk over to me. She kept talking to me, trying to keep me from passing out. Finally, my parents, Marina, and three cowboys pulled up in a car. I later learned that I had a deep gash across my forehead. My skull showed and part of my face drooped. Vince Sanchez took one look at me and said, "He's gonna die, and I'm not going to stay here and watch it happen." So he left. I heard him through my pain and my inward reaction was, "You little coyote. I'll pull through this, and when I do, I'll kick your ass."

Then I had an out-of-body experience. I was ten feet above and looking down at people milling around me. While I was there, it came to me that if I wanted to survive, I needed to take charge. Somehow, I landed back at ground level. I told one of the cowboys to call an ambulance. I knew it would take ninety minutes to arrive. I also knew I was breathing blood into my lungs because I could hear it bubble in my breathing. I was worried that I might choke to death. I told the other cowboy to get a blanket and load me in my parents' car and drive to meet the ambulance. Away we went.

Between the ranch and Duncan we met the ambulance. The EMTs transferred me and hightailed it to Safford. When I was loaded, I asked one of them if he had oxygen. Yes, he said.

"Well, get prepared to use it, because I feel like I'm going to pass out. I'll need it." Turned out I didn't pass out. I talked and talked, forcing myself to stay conscious. At the hospital, the doctor immediately ordered X-rays. Part of my hip socket had broken off, my pelvis was cracked in five places and I needed eighty stitches across my forehead. I spent the first night on some pretty heavy-duty pain meds.

The next day I turned black and blue and achy. I was in traction, stretched out across the bed. The doctor said I would be in the hospital for six weeks. I replied, "Don't count on it." Since my hips and legs were immobile, I started doing arm exercises that morning because I wasn't just going to lie there like a lump.

"How soon can I walk?" I asked the doctor next time he visited.

"How are you with pain?" he asked. I told him I could stand some. Off came the traction. I walked twenty feet with a lot of sweat and effort and in excruciating pain. Two weeks and two days later, I left the hospital.

While I was in the hospital, a representative from the Federal Aviation Administration came out to the ranch. He determined the cause of the crash that totaled the airplane: water and mud in the gas. It was the water and mud that gave the fuel its funny color. As I taxied the plane, the water settled to the bottom of the fuel tank, where it went directly into the carburetor. Motors can't run on water and mud. They quit cold.

I contacted Rex. He apologized profusely and felt just terrible. I'm sure he had a lot of insurance for such events, but I never did sue him. He was a friend, and a friend doesn't sue a friend. Years later my attorney buddy told me I could have made a small fortune on a law suit. It was six months before I could walk without pain, and my pelvis healed in a way that my toes turn out and cause me to walk duck-footed.

When I was back at the ranch and still on crutches, an old pilot named Dudley Pate called me from his home in Safford. "I have this lovely aero-plane," he said. "The same model you crashed. A Cessna 182. I want to bring it out and have you fly it."

"I certainly appreciate your offer Dudley, but I'm still healing from my last adventure." I didn't add that I wasn't sure if I would ever fly again. For certain, I was not in the mood to resume my flying career while on crutches.

But Dudley was a persistent SOB and kept calling me. "I'll fly it over to the ranch," he said each time. I grudgingly gave in, drove to the hangar for the first time since the wreck, and crutched over to his plane.

He got out of the plane and left the pilot's door open. "Hop in, Al," he said. I stowed my crutches in the back and did as I was told. He climbed in the passenger side. "Well, we're here. Let's give it a go."

I had no idea if I would freak out or have enough courage to give it the throttle. I started the engine up, taxied as I had taxied before, gave it the throttle, and took off. We actually had a nice flight. Dudley never had to take the controls. Not once did I freeze like I half-expected I would.

Later, I bought that airplane from old Dudley and flew it for years. If a horse bucks you off, climb right back on. Dudley knew that's what I needed to do. I should have thanked him, but I never did. So here's a public thank you, Dudley, for having the wisdom to talk me into doing what I didn't want to do. If you hadn't, I might not ever have flown again, and I would have missed a lot of Wildcat basketball games.

THREE HORSES

The horse lovers of the world like to think that all horses are wonderful. But horses are like people. They have different abilities, personalities, hang-ups, and ways of approaching life. Think of all the people you know. Some people are difficult to be around because of their attitude and actions. Some you can trust and some you can't. Some you love, and well, some you try to like. Often folks come into your life, and you simply have to deal with them regardless of who they are. So it has gone with horses in my life.

Take Cheyenne. He was a pretty horse, between a bay and a sorrel, with a small head and ears and an intelligent look in his eyes. Mixed in all that was a mean streak. Where it came from, I have no idea, but it sure made itself known when our cowboys started to break him. That's when

Cheyenne began looking for the opportunity to do damage to his rider.

His methodology for hurting a rider was to first get him unbalanced, then duck out from under him. If the rider fell, Cheyenne would wheel around and try to kick him, or if the rider was in range, try to bite him. Several of my cowboys got bucked off. Although I don't recall Cheyenne actually doing damage, I grew worried that he was going to succeed in his efforts, so I decided to put him in my string. Better that the boss gets hurt by a horse than someone else.

I was riding Cheyenne one day when we started rounding up in the Three Mills pasture. It was fall, and we had left headquarters at dawn, maybe around five o'clock. It was completely still that morning, but boy, was it frosty cold. About a mile and a half away, the Department of Transportation was resurfacing the highway that ran along the north side of the Three Mills pasture. As the repair crew fired up the burners to heat the asphalt, a big cloud of black smoke puffed into the air. Cheyenne took one look at that black cloud, stuck his head down, and went to bucking.

At least he bucked straight forward, so he was fairly easy to ride. The problem was that I was wearing gloves, and they were kind of old, slick gloves. Before I knew it, the reins began slipping through my hand. I had to reach higher and higher to keep the tension while Cheyenne kept bucking. My hands were just about above my head when I got to the end of the reins. They slipped right through my hands, and I tumbled backward out of the saddle. Cheyenne kicked at me with both hind feet. Fortunately, his legs weren't long enough to reach me. The other cowboys had to chase him down and bring him back to me. I was embarrassed and angry that he got the best of me. A quiet, little black cloud a mile and a half away was an awfully flimsy excuse for a horse to put his head down and go to bucking.

Another episode with Cheyenne happened at Big Tank, maybe a year later during fall roundup. It was a cold day, even colder than it had been over at Three Mills pasture. I had intestinal flu and was shivering, sweating, had diarrhea, and pretty much felt like crap. I should have taken the day off, but the boss can't take a day off on the roundup because the roundup will come to a dead stop. So there I was, wearing a big, fleece-lined coat. I had stashed a glass bottle of Kaopectate in one of the pockets.

We had ridden out before dawn and were about a mile away from Big Tank. The basalt rock, from boulders to small rocks, was everywhere, except for one spot, a circle maybe fifty yards in diameter, where Nature had left the dirt bare. When we got to that spot, my ears were freezing. The hood wasn't up on my fleece jacket because I was wearing my cowboy hat. I set my hat down on the saddle horn for a minute so I could pull up my hood. That was all Cheyenne needed. He put his head down and went to bucking. My reflexes were as sluggish as the rest of me. On the first jump, I lost the right stirrup. I thought, well, he's got me. So I started looking for a soft place to land. I hadn't even noticed that we were right in the middle of this cleared area. I thought, boy, that's lucky because I'm about to fall off, and when I come down, I won't hit a rock and the Kaopectate bottle won't break.

By then, Cheyenne decided that he'd had enough bucking. He put his head forward and started running. I had lost one bridle rein in this fiasco, so only had one bridle rein in my hand, but was able to regain my balance. He ran out of the rock-free area and charged off over the rocky prairie. I couldn't stop him because I only had the one rein, but one rein at least gives you some leverage. I pulled that rein, and sure enough, Cheyenne started making a big circle back to where the cowboys were. He pulled up to a stop in front of them. They were laughing, which I'm sure they started when Cheyenne started bucking and I was flopping all over the horse. I gathered myself back up, got my foot in the right stirrup, found the other rein, eventually got my hat, and on we went.

I rode Cheyenne for quite some time after that. I never did like him because I never did trust him. I was pretty certain he'd hurt me given the chance. But he was a strong horse and could get the job done as long as I kept my guard up and didn't have the flu.

Another horse that bucked a lot, though for different reasons, was a mare we raised at the ranch named Idiot. I don't remember her mother or the cowboy who bequeathed her that name. Idiot was nervous all her life. When she was just a filly and we were teaching her to lead and load in the trailer, she was goosey and jumpy and hard to deal with. When you got your hand on her and talked sweet to her, she calmed down. She loved to be rubbed and would put her head down and beg you to keep rubbing on her. If you did anything that was a new or fast movement, she jumped and whirled and tried to jerk loose and run off. Unlike Cheyenne, she didn't want to hurt anyone. She was just nervous.

By the time she was a young mare and big enough to be broken, we had too many horses on the ranch. DA didn't want to increase our mare herd so he picked five fillies to be spayed, and she was one. He said go ahead and break them, they'll make good saddle horses.

I assigned Idiot to Lonnie Moore, a young cowboy from Duncan who was working at the ranch. Lonnie took her, but was always afraid of her. I didn't blame him. She was so jumpy, Lonnie was afraid that she was going to jump out from under him. If a jackrabbit jumped out real close to her or under her feet, she jumped about ten feet forward instead of jumping sideways away from the rabbit. When you got on her, she stood still and waited, then started off nicely until you moved your weight wrong, or your hat blew off, or you swung your arm out suddenly to point to a cow. Then she jumped like she'd seen a rabbit or coyote, and she'd try to get away. Sometimes she ran off. If you didn't pull up on her pretty quick, she kept on going.

One day we were at High Lonesome and had just started to drive some cattle toward Summit. Lonnie was riding Idiot. He dismounted to take off his jacket. Using the saddle string, he tied part of the jacket on the left side of the saddle. Before Lonnie could secure the jacket on the other side, it flopped against Idiot's right side. She jerked loose from Lonnie and ran about four miles before we could catch her. The only thing that frightened her was that loose jacket. Lonnie started calling her Wanda. He said, "You wanda what the hell she's going to do next."

I decided to start riding Wanda. I figured one of the cowboys would get careless and get bucked off or fall off, get their boot hung in the stirrup and get dragged, or somehow get hurt. After my first of couple rides, I learned that I had to sit right square in the center of her back and not wave my arms or shift my weight. Then she acted like a really good cow horse. I also learned she was super strong. She had muscles like iron. I could ride her on my longest days when we covered twenty-five miles. She was the same when I got on her first thing in the morning as she was eight or ten hours later. A lot of horses weaken toward the end of a long day. You hope they don't get so tired that they quit you. But Wanda was always fresh and strong and was a real pleasure to ride on a long day. She walked through the deep rocks like an athlete. She had exceptional balance and could step over larger rocks and find a spot to put her feet between the small rocks and never slow down.

She didn't mind a rope too much. She was nervous when I swung the rope, but if I roped a calf and went to drag it to the branding fire, she knew her business and would go to the fire. If the calf ever started running toward her with the rope, or especially ran behind her where the rope touched her hips or under her tail, she blew up like a stick of dynamite. I didn't want to be on her when that happened. I roped a lot of calves and dragged them to the branding fire, but boy, oh boy, was I careful not to let them have any slack or let them run up behind her.

One time, I was riding her on the longest day of the round-up. The wind was blowing that day, a big old west wind blowing thirty miles an hour all day. The drive down to Old Camp went fine. When we turned east and began the trek back home, the wind at our backs, Wanda started jumping and whirling and kicking and was just very upset with something. I couldn't figure out what it was. Several times I dismounted and examined things. I finally discovered a bunch of cockleburs caught in her tail. When we headed east, the wind blew her tail up between her legs and the cockleburs scratched her. She wasn't having any of that. I took out my pocketknife and cut off her tail right below the end of the bone. The bone runs down the center of the tail, then stops. Below that point, tail hairs hang down for another foot or two. So I cut her tail off at the end of the bone and didn't leave any cockleburs.

I rode Wanda for many years. We got along fine and had a good partnership. She told me what she expected from me, and I always tried to give it to her by not getting lazy with my posture or hand motions. Then I could count on her to be a mighty fine cow horse, loyal and trustworthy to the end.

Another fine cow horse I had was Little Charlie Brown. I was starting to cowboy full-time when Little Charlie came along. He was the younger brother of Charlie Brown, another good cow horse. The two looked quite alike. Little Charlie was gentle, had a good gait, and loved to work cattle. When you were cutting cattle in the herd, you were happy when you were riding Little Charlie.

He had two characteristics that set him apart from other horses. When Little Charlie and I rode in the drag, if a cow slowed, Little Charlie charged that cow and bit her muscle right above the back hock. He clamped down so hard that he raised that cow's leg clear off the ground. The cow would bawl and jump and try to run, but she couldn't get far with her leg firmly stuck between Little Charlie's jaws. I'm sure it hurt. If I spurred him, he held on to it for twenty or thirty yards. The cow kicked at Little Charlie with her free leg, but he held his head sideways and dodged the kicks. If I pulled back, his teeth came off the cow's muscle with a snap. That cow usually didn't drop to the back any more because it wasn't pleasant to get her leg bitten. Driving cattle that way was fun because Little Charlie kept the herd moving. He never bit a calf, though, only nudged it. I didn't teach him to do that. Somehow he knew not to hurt a baby. He just bumped the little guy with his nose and boosted him forward.

The other thing I always loved about Little Charlie Brown was his strength. He wasn't a very big horse, but by golly, could he pull, and by that I mean he could drag about anything I roped. If I had a full-grown bull roped and needed it dragged into the next corral or somewhere, I'd dally up, and Little Charlie would do his thing. He'd crouch low to the ground, tuck his head, and lurch forward. Most of the horses couldn't do that. They'd pull at that bull and pull and pull until I'd know they couldn't get the job done. I never really figured out how a horse as small as Little Charlie developed so much power. He must have had the right kind of muscles. If you were roping calves and dragging them to the fire for branding, you could rope all day long and Little Charlie would never tire. Most horses will tell you they're getting tired after dragging fifteen or twenty calves, and it needs to be somebody else's turn. But not Little Charlie. I could rope on him all day.

He was one of my favorite horses because he had those fun personality traits. When he wasn't driving cattle or pulling something, he could be a little lazy. He acted like he was half asleep. But when I got my rope out, he became all horse. I always was really happy to saddle up with Little Charlie because when I did, I could trust him to give the two of us a good day.

CIRCLES OF TRUST

anch children learn how to drive at an early age. So it went with my sisters and me. Since we never drove underage on the highway, we never broke any laws. Our first driving lesson was sitting on DA's lap and steering the pickup. Ann and I loved that, but then we wanted to learn how to shift, so he taught us how to shift. He pushed in the clutch and one of us shifted the gears. It would be some time, however, before either of us would be tall enough to work the clutch. So at ages six and five, Ann and I became determined to figure out a way to drive the pickup together without DA's help.

We worked out a system. I crawled on the floorboard where I was responsible for pushing the clutch, the brake, or the accelerator. Ann steered, shifted, and told me which pedals to push. At first, we only were allowed to do this when DA was in the pickup with us. After a time, he began letting us drive through open gates on our own. He got out of the pickup, opened the gate, and Ann and I drove through without him. That was the coolest—not having him in the truck.

One day we stopped at a large gate going into Big Pasture and DA got out to open it.

"Let the clutch out," Ann said.

I did. We rolled through the gate. I was waiting for her to say brake, but the command never came. We weren't going fast, but we were going. I saw her look over her shoulder.

"Speed up," she said. She started to giggle.

I followed orders.

"He's catching up. Go faster!" said Ann. Now she was laughing. I was thinking that DA would soon be shooting fire from his hat. We bounced over the ground some more. Finally, Ann started circling back. When I sat up, we were in front of DA, who had his hands on his hips and his hat on the ground. He had run about a hundred yards. By then, Ann and I were doubled-over and laughing so hard that he couldn't help but see the humor and join in.

By the time I turned thirteen, I was a seasoned ranch-road driver. We had about sixty miles of road on Lazy B, and I knew every mile of it. A classmate of mine owned a '34 Plymouth and wanted to get rid of it, so I bought it from him for seventy-five dollars. It was a classy car, a deep green, single-seater convertible with a rumble seat and spoked wheels. What thirteen-year-old wouldn't be in high-heaven with that car? Its speed topped out at about sixty miles per hour. DA made me promise that I would never run it on the highway, and I never did. He also forbade me to use ranch gas. I talked the distributor who brought gas to the ranch into bringing a barrel for me. I paid him every time. Each barrel lasted me quite awhile.

When I went to college, I bought another car, one with a license, and left the Plymouth at the ranch. During a semester break, I went looking for the Plymouth only to discover DA had sold it. He was tired of having that old car around. I was heartbroken. I had loved it, and now it was gone. DA never gave me the money from the sale and never told me to whom he'd sold it. He pulled stunts like that every so often. But he was my father and I felt like I needed to trust him (or work around him), and always hoped he trusted me.

I had a different relationship with my mother. We implicitly trusted each other. In her later years, MO suffered from dementia. Sandra, Ann, and I had a family meeting where we decided that I could care for her best at the ranch in the familiar surroundings she loved so much.

I loved having MO at the ranch. Every day, she waited for me to come in from work, then asked me the same question: "Can we go for a walk?"

We set out on our walk, and for the half-mile or sometimes mile, I told her about my day. She didn't always talk about hers, but often commented on the birds and other animals we might see or on the cacti and other plants. We appreciated our time together and being outdoors.

One day in late summer, I walked in and she said, "Can we go for a walk?"

I said, "Look at the clouds outside. I don't think it's a good idea to walk today. It looks like it's about to rain."

"I think we should go ahead and walk," she countered.

I let her twist my arm. We started out walking and watching the clouds. We barely were a quarter mile from the house when a cloud decided to turn itself loose. Big hard raindrops fell on us.

When we started to get seriously wet, I picked up MO like you would a child. She didn't weigh but a hundred pounds. She wrapped her arms around my neck, and I went running back toward the house. I'll never forget her laughter. She was having the best time that she could imagine. We arrived completely soaked, but both giggling at our experience. It was one of the best walks I've ever taken. If she hadn't trusted me to care for her, and if neither of us had trusted that things would work out, we never would have had those special times together.

CHAPTER 29

STITCHED UP

Healthcare on ranches is sometimes homespun. In our community, the only doctor was Doc Loveitt, who wasn't always home. Since the nearest hospital was sixty miles away, we learned to do minor cowboy doctoring. I took the cast off my nephew's arm a few weeks early because it smelled godawful. I pulled more prickers and thorns from myself and others than I could possibly count. Almost every day, either my foreman or I did veterinary work on our cattle and horses.

One day over lunch, Jim Brister came to me saying that his tooth hurt. Would I look in his mouth? I did and saw a huge cavity in the center of a back molar. I told him that he needed to go to the dentist. He kind of smiled and said, "I can handle this." He went to the barn, got a new piece of baling wire, bent it into an L-shape, came back to the bunkhouse, went to the stove, and started heating the end of the wire. I sat there drinking coffee. He heated that wire until it got red hot. Then he opened his mouth and inserted it in his cavity. It sizzled and smoked and sweat poured off his brow, but he never flinched. I was having to fight down nausea. He set the wire down and said, "That takes care of that," and walked out the door. Hardscrabble cowboys don't go to the dentist for root canals. And sometimes they don't go to the doctor for stitches.

Number one and only son was breaking horses as a teenager and decided to mount one bareback. The horse spooked and ran off with him. It ran up to a six-wire barbed fence and turned back, but number one son didn't turn back and landed with his back in the barbed wire. He came to the house a little later with a ripped and bloody shirt and two cuts on his back a quarter-inch deep and about five-inches long where the barbed wire had done its intended use.

I said, "Al, you need to go get that stitched up."

He said, "Well Dad, it's the weekend and Doc Loveitt is probably gone, and I don't want to be hauled to town anyway. So why don't you make some butterfly bandages and use those?"

I finally agreed. I found a box full of band-aids and modified them to a butterfly shape. I put six on each cut to hold the cut together. To this day, Al has the scars left to prove it.

A few years later, Al was selling desert plants to wholesale nurseries in Phoenix. It was Saturday and he had taken a load of seven hundred five-gallon pots of creosote bushes, triple-decked in the truck, to Phoenix. The old truck we had for that purpose should have been retired years before, but we were still using it. He was halfway back to the ranch that evening when the transmission came unbolted and fell onto the frame. The truck stopped. Al pulled over, crawled under the truck, and found the problem. Fortunately, he also found a couple of bolts in the toolbox that we kept in the cab. So he jacked the transmission into place and tightened the bolts. When he crawled out from under the truck after finishing the job, he stood up not realizing the driver's door was open. He gashed his head on the bottom corner of the door. Blood started running everywhere. He got into the truck and drove the final fifty miles with blood dripping onto his shirt and shoulders. When he walked into the house, I didn't know if he was my son or a character from a horror film, he looked so bad.

"This one has to be stitched up," I said. "It's too deep and too big."

He replied, "Doc Loveitt is out of state on vacation." In a small town, everybody knows everybody's business. "Besides, Dad, I've seen you stitch up a lot of cows and horses. Why don't you just stitch me up?"

I didn't really want to, but it was almost midnight, and we were looking at a sixty-mile drive to the hospital and there was no guarantee that a doctor would be on duty. I had several curved needles that I used for sewing up cattle, so I fetched one from the barn and got some dental floss for the stitching material. I sterilized the needle as best as I could and shaved around the edge of the cut. I poured a double shot of vodka and told Al to drink it. Then I put eight of the prettiest stitches in the top of his head. He never flinched or cried out, but I'm sure it was painful.

He drove back to college the next day. His girlfriend was a nurse. She looked at the wound and said, "You either need to send your dad to jail for practicing medicine without a license or send him a blue ribbon because this is a nice job." She took the stitches out later, and they didn't even leave a scar.

That was my crowning achievement as a ranch doctor. I never lost a patient and haven't had one since.

CHAPTER 30

WATERMELON THIEVES

It was August, and Lazy B was baking like beans. I was playing Big Uncle Al to seven kids—my two plus four nephews and a niece. We had finished a fence job and it was a slack moment. These kids need some fun, I thought. What entertainment can I cough up? We were near the river, always good for a splash. I remember plenty of times as a kid running into the water to cool off, clothes and all, like the time Rastus and I ran in after eating watermelon. It took about three minutes for us to dry. Rastus had taken me on rounds with him to check the cattle, and we had ended up near a watermelon patch. Rastus asked me if I wanted to get some watermelon. What ranch kid doesn't love watermelon? We walked into the watermelon field, and Rastus grabbed a watermelon big enough to feed him, me, and the entire crew. Or so I thought. When I started to follow him, he stopped. "Get your own melon," he said. "This one's mine." So I picked one as big as my six-year-old self could handle. We settled in the shade of some cottonwoods, and he pulled out his knife, cut his melon lengthwise, then handed me the knife. I cut my first watermelon right there. We both dug into the heart, the ripe, seedless center. I never had the luxury of eating a whole watermelon by myself, and of course I couldn't, but it sure was fun trying. That's what these kids needed—a watermelon experience. And maybe a juiced-up one at that.

"Hey, I've got a great idea," I said. "How'd you like to go down near the Gila River, steal a few watermelons, and go eat them under the cottonwoods?" Their screams startled the cows lolling by the fence.

Everyone loaded into the pickup, and we bounced over ranch road to the watermelon patch. I rented out twenty acres to Andy Jensen who had planted watermelons on them. "Any time you want some," he said, "come get 'em." I stopped at the far end of a field full of beautiful, ripe watermelons.

"All right, here's the deal," I said before the letting the kids out of the truck. "The farmer who owns this field is a real mean dude. I hear he loads his shotgun with salt, and if he sees you stealing watermelons, he'll shoot you." Seven sets of eyebrows arched. "So we have to be quiet and quick out there. Pick two, and high-tail it back here."

With giggles and anticipation, our gang of thieves crept low into the field. All the kids could heft one watermelon under each arm, except for Jay. At six years old, he was the youngest and could only manage one. I made sure everyone had their melons, then pointed to the truck. We started the return trek juggling the fruit and snickering. I turned around to make sure everyone was in tow. Jay held up the rear. He was a pudgy little thing and his melon looked to be half his size. We all arrived back and set down our heavy load except for Jay, still a good fifty feet away waddling along with his melon.

Being the loving uncle, I started shouting encouragement. "Come on, Jay. I see the farmer coming and he's likely to shoot you. So hurry! Run fast!"

Jay started to run. As he did, his pants fell down around his knees, hobbling him. He couldn't pull his pants up without putting down the watermelon, and he couldn't run holding the watermelon. The other kids, quick to catch on, joined in with encouragement.

"Here he comes, Jay."

"Get outta there. Fast!"

Jay waddled a few steps forward.

"Hurry, Jay! Just keep running."

"You can do it."

Suddenly Jay stopped. A distinct change came over him. It was as if he concluded, if I'm caught, I'm caught. I can't do a thing about it. He deliberately set down the watermelon, pulled up his pants, and secured them. Then he picked up the big melon, settled it in his arms and with great dignity, walked over to the fence where the rest of us were howling with laughter.

We carted the melons to the cottonwoods by the river. I pulled out my knife and carved mine, showing them where the heart was, and passed the knife around. We ate our hearts out, feeling like we had gotten away with something. I fessed up about the farmer, and we laughed and giggled some more while sweet, pink juice dribbled down our chins. Then we ran down to the river and jumped in with our clothes on. It felt good and cooling as always. I had a feeling Rastus was looking down at us that day, smiling, a big old slice of watermelon in his hand.

~PART 7~

ON ENDINGS

Live a good honorable life, then, when you get older
and look back on it, you'll enjoy it a second time.

CHAPTER 31

LETTY

My wife's grandmother, Letty, was one of the most interesting characters I've ever known. She was born and raised in a polygamist family in one of the Mormon colonies in Chihuahua, Mexico. When the Mormons moved west, one branch migrated to Mexico, where there weren't laws against polygamy. As soon as she turned fourteen, Letty was married off to an older polygamist man. One night she went to a dance; with or without her husband, she never said. A young man about her age also decided to attend. Letty danced one dance with him. Almost before the song ended, he declared his love for Letty and suggested they run away together. Letty was unhappy that she'd been dealt-off to a fifty-year-old, so she readily agreed to the proposition.

Late that night, the young man scratched on her window. Letty opened it and made her escape. They had one horse and rode double through the night and into the next day, finally stopping for a few hours in an abandoned ranch shack. Her escape-mate cautioned that they could only stay a few hours because folks from the colony would certainly be after them. After their brief rest, they rode almost non-stop to the border at Douglas, Arizona, where they crossed into the United States. They promptly got married and lived happily together for sixty-five years.

Letty had many fascinating tales about her life and was a marvelous storyteller. I would sit at her feet and listen to her talk about the big life she lived. When she was about eight-years-old, Pancho Villa and his army invaded her small town and stayed a good while before going on their nefarious way. During this time, Letty's mother had one strict rule that absolutely couldn't be broken: Letty had to be home by sunset. One afternoon, Letty was playing in a field. When she looked up, she realized that she had two minutes until sunset. She took off running for home as fast as she could go. To get there, she had to run across a board that spanned an irrigation ditch. As she started across the board, she could see Pancho Villa and his bodyguard coming across the board toward her. She didn't care. She was in a race with the sun, and more afraid of her strict mother than she was of the Mexican general. She ran pell-mell onto the bridge and knocked the bodyguard into the water. Pancho Villa roared with laughter. Letty made it home and was not punished.

A couple of years later, Pancho Villa returned to dip into the town's supply base. He took beef and apples, horses and cattle, and he left a wounded colonel. The colonel had been wounded for some time and was at death's door. Pancho Villa declared that someone in the house needed to nurse the colonel back to health. He chose Letty. Did he remember her from crossing the board? She was never certain. She told Pancho Villa that she knew nothing about medicine and furthermore, there was none in the house. Pancho Villa replied that if the colonel didn't heal, it would go very badly for Letty's family. Not knowing what else to do, Letty took some flour and cloth, made a poultice, and put it on the colonel's wound. The colonel fully recovered. Pancho Villa was so impressed that he insisted Letty serve as a nurse in his army. She went, though not willingly. After a year of service, she returned to the colony. Shortly after, she was married off to the older polygamist man.

Letty died at the age of ninety-six. The family asked me to speak at her funeral. I was honored by the request because I had such huge respect for Letty and the courageous, loving life she had lived. The funeral was held at a church in Safford, Arizona. Over one hundred people attended, including Letty's half-sister, who also was ninety-six. She sat in a front row chair. At the appropriate point in the service, I stepped up to the front and began speaking. I was about midway through my prepared remarks when Letty's half-sister put her hand over her heart, cried out, "Oh Letty!" and fell over. When she hit the floor, I knew she was dead. Just knew it.

Someone called 911, and the funeral came to a halt. The ambulance arrived and transported Letty's sister to the nearest hospital. Everyone was a bit shaken. I was asked to return to the front of the church and continue speaking. Somehow I managed to stumble forward with my story. After the service, we all went to the cemetery to bury Letty. As we arrived, word spread that Letty's sister had indeed died.

I was honored to have been a very small part of Letty's life and was able to share her life story. But that was the last time I spoke at a funeral. You've heard of people who are so boring they bore you to death? Not wanting further damage weighing on my conscience, I vowed never to give another eulogy. Fortunately for others, I've kept that vow and never intend to break it.

CHAPTER 32

SYLVESTER & SUSIE

I've had a lot of animal friends over the years, but two of my favorites were indoor pets. Just thinking about them still makes me smile.

During roundup one spring, I noticed a little bird on the ground flopping this way and that. He looked different from a dove or quail, so I got off my horse to take a closer look. I could tell by the downward curve of the beak that the little fellow was a hawk, a baby hawk. Based on its coloring, it looked to be a sparrow hawk. If it lived, it would grow to be the size of a dove.

I put the little guy in my glove and put the glove in my shirt pocket. By the time I arrived home, he was pretty bedraggled. My wife Barbara took an instant liking to him. She found some raw meat and fed him, and he gobbled it up like there was no tomorrow. Immediately, the two bonded. She named him Sylvester.

Sylvester learned that when he squawked, one of us would come running with food. For days, he ate ravenously. He came to trust both of us and would hop up on our arm or especially a shoulder and ride around like he was king of the house. He grew rapidly and before long, he was trying to fly.

I took over as his flight instructor. We had a big living room, and he would go careening around it and bounce off the walls and the couch. He had more crashes than I ever did. Fortunately, he was never hurt. Soon he was flying around the living room like it was his own private airport. He was ready for his next lesson: outdoor flight.

I took Sylvester outside and let him go. He flew around for a bit, then came screeching back to me. He was a natural. He started taking daily solo flights, some long, some short. After each, he'd land on my shoulder or head and, with much ado, tell me about his adventures of where he'd been and what he'd done. I always knew by the tone of his squawks whether he was happy or unhappy. When he was flying, I could call him, and he'd come to me like a missile. As he grew, he developed the most vivid green and brown feathers around his neck. He was just beautiful.

Sylvester never was house trained, so that was a bit of a problem. When he sat on my shoulder, he messed up the back of my shirt. It was a small price to pay for the love and happiness that he brought with him. I built a perch for him on the outdoor porch, which he used as home base. What he especially liked was to be on top of the huge windmill that was the centerpiece of the ranch. I'd walk out on the porch and call him, and here he'd come. I always had fresh meat in my hand, and he knew what to expect.

When Sylvester was about eight months old, he started leaving for a day or two, then would come back. I knew he was getting ready to shove off for good. I hated the thought. Sure enough, one day he up and left. We were his first family, but the time had come for him to find his second one. I like to think he circled the ranch one last time, raised a wing, and flew away. To this day we still talk about Sylvester and his funny antics and loving personality.

The other pet embedded in Day family history is Susie, the dog we had while I was growing up. She was a little short-legged, barrel-chested dog. She had short, white hair and a tail that curled over her back. I think she was a stray that Sandra found on the ranch. Susie was the only dog allowed in the house. These privileges were granted her when I was too young to know that not every dog received special treatment. When she looked at you, you could read the intelligence in her eyes. She fit in our family like a fourth child.

Susie loved all the family equally and would always come when called. Every morning, she made it a point to visit each family member in bed and greet him or her with a smile. If you didn't know better, you'd think her smile was a snarl, but it wasn't. She'd pull back her lips, stick out her tongue, and hiss.

Susie wasn't spoiled and never was in the way, yet she was always part of any event in the house. One of her best traits was that she could hear cars coming up the ranch road when they still were several miles away. She'd give a couple of little barks. You could always tell whether it was a stranger or a ranch vehicle by her bark. If we heard a stranger bark, we would say company's coming, and my mother would make a fresh pot of coffee and get ready to receive guests.

Susie only had one enemy—the pig we kept down in the corral. Once a day, the pig would visit the back of the bunkhouse to eat the cowboys' table scraps. When that pig took one step out of the corral, Susie would jump up from her nap and have a barking tantrum.

I loved having Susie as a companion. I'd take her with me to check the windmills or put out salt licks for the cattle. She loved to come along. I almost always took a 22 rifle to shoot jackrabbits. They ate a lot of grass that I wanted for the cows. Susie would spot the jackrabbits first and would tell me where they were. I'd stop and shoot the rabbit. She'd then jump out of the jeep and land on her head because her legs were short. She'd pick herself up and run over to the jackrabbit, shake it to death, then strut back to the jeep, so proud of herself for being such a great hunter. Sometimes she would get a little blood on her chest or leg. She'd make sure to show me the badge of courage that she earned while shaking that mean rabbit.

Susie lived a long and healthy life. When she finally got old and passed, it was one of the saddest days we had on the ranch. I was a senior in high school. Of course, I missed her. Terribly. But when I think of her, I don't think of the missing. I think of all the fun we had and feel grateful that she was a part of my life.

CHAPTER 33

BEEF JERKY

"Hey, Uncle Al, have you started the jerky yet?"

My nephew Jay looked at me from across the table. I swallowed my mouthful of Thanksgiving Day turkey, but before I could respond, his brothers chimed in with their requests for the cowboy delicacy. The requests for jerky usually start about Thanksgiving. It's the only Christmas gift I give and those on my list don't seem to want to wait until then to dip into their present.

"Guess I better get on that," I said. Of course I wouldn't have said anything else. I've been making jerky for way too long to admit. I learned the trade in middle school from one of the Lazy B cowboys. He had a rudimentary process: slice the beef with a sharp knife, season it with salt and pepper, and loop the long, thin slices over the clothesline to dry in the Arizona sun for three or four days. The flies would find it, of course, so when the strips came off the line, you were never sure if you were eating pepper or flyspecks, but no one much cared. The finished product ended up in a pillowcase propped up on a chair in the bunkhouse. No one could pass by without sticking a hand into that grab bag. The salty leathery beef tasted especially good on horseback while out on the range driving cattle. If you're supposed to chew your food thirty times, you had to chew that jerky at least three times longer.

After the cowboy left Lazy B, I took over the reins of jerky making. The main house had an oil stove, so rather than hanging the meat on a clothesline, I put it on trays underneath the stove to dry. I started experimenting with different seasonings—teriyaki, then habanero chilies, and hot sauce. I'd throw the seasonings in a pot and let them simmer into a mouthwatering concoction. Every year, the concoction got a little tastier. I'd put the jerky in baggies for the crew and during the month of December, we'd all keep a stash in our chaps.

When I moved to Tucson, I convinced the meat lab at the University of Arizona, to slice and dry the meat for me. I supplied the sweet-n-salty hot sauce. The interns would dip the meat in it and put the slices in the dehydrator. I started selling the jerky commercially, but after a few years the endeavor required more time than I wanted to devote to it, so I purchased a commercial slicer and a dehydrator that holds a dozen or so trays. Now I'm a one-stop, beef-jerky-making shop, but only during the Christmas season. It's a gift I make with my own hands, and no one can duplicate it because I've never given away the secret ingredients in the sauce.

When I sold Lazy B, one of the things I brought with me was my jerky making. Every time I smell that sauce, I'm back on Lazy B. The jerky has meaning for me.

When Sandra moved to Washington to be a justice on the Supreme Court, she couldn't find any Mexican restaurants there with the right spices in the food. So I sent her a big bag of jerky, so she could have her taste of hot sauce. It became an annual ritual. After several years, she reported to me that she always shared it on Fridays with the other justices, several of whom had never tasted jerky. After I heard that, I made a rather large sack and sent it to the court with a note:

My sister tells me that you justices enjoy the beef jerky. As you probably know, cowboys use jerky on long rides. But a little known fact is that by eating jerky, they believe they become smarter. I hope it works for the court.

I received an amazing response.

January 16, 1997
    Dear Mr. Day, Home on the range again; you got us as close to it as you could, anyway, when your big sister delivered the hoard of great beef jerky. We take a lot in this

job and lucky for us that some of it comes from you. The court is unanimous. Many, many thanks from all of us.

William Rehnquist
Anthony Kennedy
Stephen Breyer
David Souter
John Paul Stevens
Clarence Thomas
Ruth Bader Ginsberg
Antonin Scalia

CHAPTER 34

LEAVING LAZY B

I had been managing Lazy B for close to forty years. During those four decades, I never once considered being anything but a rancher. It was a job I absolutely loved. I had assumed my son or one of my five nephews would step up and take the management reins. They all loved Lazy B and spent a lot of time there, especially in the summers. I think there's a romantic fantasy that ranch life plays out like a John Wayne movie. Alan Jr. and his cousins knew firsthand the effort required to run a ranch. Now in their thirties and early forties, most of them had established careers in business, teaching, real estate and other entrepreneurial endeavors. Only one nephew had chosen the cowboy life.

After that nephew graduated from college, he came to work at Lazy B. He had learned cowboying at an early age, but he also needed to learn the ranching side of cowboying. I insisted he come up to the office one day a week for a lesson in ranch business. It turned out that administrative duties didn't agree with him. After he left to cowboy on another ranch, I discovered a bunch of neglected paperwork stuffed in his desk drawer. That's when I finally had to admit that the lineage of Lazy B managers stopped with me. It was a hard pill to swallow.

For months, I agonized about what to do. Should I stay at Lazy B and hang on as long as I was able? Or should my partners and I sell while I was still capable of doing other things, whatever those things might be? I knew a handful of old ranchers who hung on too long because their kids weren't interested in taking over. They eventually had trouble mounting a horse and couldn't do the horseback work they once did. Angry with their heirs, they became curmudgeons. The last thing I wanted to be was a curmudgeon rancher.

I decided to call a meeting at Lazy B with my partners—Sandra, Ann, and my cousin Don. I dreaded the meeting. I gave a lot of thought to what I was going to say. I didn't want to tell them that our way of life was evaporating. None of them had walked in my shoes, sat in my office chair, or contemplated the future. To them, the future was all about therapeutic visits to the ranch. While I loved working with my hands and with the livestock, I also had unpleasant tasks, the biggest of which involved dealing with the Bureau of Land Management. Seventy-six percent of Lazy B was federal land that we leased for grazing. During the past four decades, the local BLM office had grown from five employees to one hundred fifty. Someone at some level was dreaming up regulations to make ranching tougher; more than a few of those regulations were ridiculous. I always had maintained good relationships with the BLM, but I no longer enjoyed working with the agency.

The day of the partners' meeting, I explained the BLM's ways. Then I described what the prospects were of continuing to own the ranch. The price of the ranch wasn't going to increase because so much of the land was leased. Operating expenses would continue to rise while income would remain static. Every year, I grew older. The clock was ticking. Even though we didn't owe money and made an annual profit, the future didn't look particularly bright. Sandra especially became angry. For about two hours, I suffered her slings and arrows. I couldn't blame her. It felt like our heritage and the place that formed us and was important to us was slipping away. She vented. Finally, though unwillingly, she said that she accepted the truth of what I was saying. After further extended discussion, we agreed that the pragmatic answer was to sell Lazy B. It had been one hundred and ten years since our grandfather settled on the ranch. When the meeting disbanded, the mood was dismal and tearful. We informed the rest of the family. Of course, they were sad, but they accepted our decision.

I contacted Fred Baker, the most respected ranch broker in Arizona. He came out to Lazy B and spent quite a little time with me on the ranch and in the office. Together, we priced the ranch and packaged the prospectus. Then, we tried to sell it for two years. Fred showed it ten times and had no bids. Most buyers said they weren't looking for such a big ranch. Two years was a graduate course in discouragement.

I went back to square one. I pulled out maps of the ranch and based on its geography, divided the land into five parcels. I offered each parcel for sale, with the stipulation that the outlying parcels had to sell first and headquarters sell last. Buyers soon stepped up with opened checkbooks. Seeing the ranch shrink was spirit-draining. A year later, only the headquarters unit was still for sale.

Gary Overmann, a rancher from Nevada, came back a bunch of times to look at the headquarters. For years, he owned a ranch in the desert between Las Vegas and the California border. The entire ranch was on government-leased land. When the BLM learned that the endangered Mojave tortoises shared the space, the agency proposed taking the land away from Gary and giving it to the tortoises. The ranch appraised at ten million dollars. The deal was that Congress would appropriate the money to buy the ranch and save the tortoises, and Gary would walk away with ten million bucks. So Gary, banking on a windfall from the government, secured private financing and purchased the last section of Lazy B.

Gary was proud of his way of ranching. His definition of success was to squeeze a profit out of the ranch with little regard for the grass and cattle. He never worked on fences and seldom on wells and even lived without electricity. He kept overhead so low that all of his sales of calves went into the profit side of the ledger. My definition of success was excess grass and fat cattle. Lazy B was an ongoing operation with overhead. I paid attention to fencing, pipelines, and wells, and had cowboys on the payroll, things Gary had no interest in. But no one anointed me caretaker and teacher of the next generation of management.

It was time let it all go and let the next guy have his turn. That next guy, whether I liked it or not, was Gary.

I suddenly felt rudderless. My wife and I would be moving, but where were we supposed to go? I didn't want to move to Phoenix or Denver or El Paso or Albuquerque. My wife Sue didn't like the ranch in South Dakota, so we couldn't move there. Besides, winters up north were mighty cold. The only other place I had lived was Tucson. By default, Tucson became our new home. I was still busy with the South Dakota ranch and also wrapping up details at Lazy B, so I told Sue to go buy a house. She said, "I don't know what you like." I said, "I don't either." My only criterion was to buy a house that would be easy to resell. I figured after we lived in town for a bit, we'd know what we liked and needed. I was pretty certain our first house wouldn't be our forever house.

The dreaded day finally arrived. I turned my mind on autopilot. I loaded furniture and clothes in a trailer that I borrowed from Gary, a trailer that I once owned and sold to him. I cleaned up the empty house. I kept moving. Neither Sandra nor Ann called. Sue was in Tucson getting the new house ready. As the day progressed, it felt more and more surreal. It was as if life were tripping by; I didn't feel connected to any of it.

At last, I was packed and ready to leave. Gary asked me where the key was to the front door. "I don't know," I said. "We've never had a key." In all the years that I'd lived at Lazy B, I never locked the front door. Nor had I taken a key out of a car or pickup. We always left the keys in the console of any vehicle so the next driver didn't have to hunt them down. Right then, I realized that I would need to learn to live in a different way. I got in my pickup, pointed it down the eight-mile ranch road, and drove away from the only home and lifestyle I'd ever known. I wept the entire way down that road and well past Lordsburg.

Just before sundown, I arrived at our new Tucson home. I backed the thirty-foot horse trailer still covered with manure up to the house and started unloading what furniture I could carry. The next day, I found a homeowners' association letter stuck in the front door. Horse trailers are not allowed, it said. The following day, I hung a piece of colorful art over the garage. Two days letter, another HOA letter arrived informing me that I could only hang colorful art on the back of the house. It took me less than a week to figure out where I didn't want to live.

Then, the biggest change hit with the force of a monsoon cloudburst. During my entire ranching career, I woke up in the morning knowing that the chore list was longer than the hours in the day. Sometimes I wished for a twin. But now, living in town, I only had one thing to do each day and that was to figure out how to occupy my day. For a week, I bumbled and fumbled around and drove Sue crazy. Adding to my discomfort was my bank account. For the first time in my life, I had a large chunk of change in the bank and it frightened me something terrible. Ranchers have their money tied up in land, cattle, and equipment. I had managed large assets but personally never had much cash on hand. If I invested it poorly, it would disappear, leaving me with nothing to show for forty years of hard work. It was one scary time.

At the start of the second week, I decided to go down to Habit for Humanity and see if I could make myself useful.

Turned out nobody was a fix-it guy for the inhabitants of new homes. Habitat loved me. I could speak Spanish. I was a self-starter. And I could fix shit. It didn't take long before I was going around to newly completed houses, my toolbox in hand, replacing circuit breakers, fixing sinks, drip systems, you name it. I was one of two people authorized to use the organization's credit card to buy materials. Every weekday, I worked for Habitat on my own schedule. One thing I did was create a punch list for the foreman in charge of jobs, which could be used to troubleshoot problems prior to people moving in. Nobody had ever created one. Alan Jr. was building houses at the time and I simply borrowed his punch list. The problems facing new owners began to decrease. After a year, I ended my small, but satisfying career.

I visited the Lazy B two or three times during the first few years after selling it. Gary let the fences fall down and didn't charge the electric fences. He left all the gates open and let the cows wander. We had kept meticulous well records about every well—how deep it was, what repairs had been done. There was a log on all thirty-five wells. When I told Gary that those records would really help him out, he nodded in agreement. But then he tossed them out. All of them! For one thing, he couldn't read and write. For another, he used a well maintenance guy, and we never did. In addition, I strongly urged him not to buy any new cows for two years. Right away, he purchased five hundred cows. I could see the grass thinning. Talk about having your heart eaten out. Mother Nature dealt him some bad luck. The day I sold the ranch the ranch, the rain stopped. It was the start of five bad years of rain. After four years, Gary's private investor foreclosed on him. I wasn't surprised. That investor still owns the ranch.

My passion for the ranch, the horses, the grass—all that was my life—continues. Now, I express that passion through writing, which in turn brings me great joy. While I lived on the ranch, I often thought I was luckiest guy I know. Leaving that way of life was sad and daunting. But I've come to realize that if I'd allowed my disappointment in ending my ranching and wild horse careers to take over my life, I would've missed the new adventures and new experiences that continue to land in my lap, just as they always did at Lazy B. It's hard to predict what roads we'll end up traveling in life and what lessons we'll learn during our journeys. About the best we can do is sit up straight in the saddle, keep an eye on the trail, learn from the tough times, and be grateful for the good times. For me, the sun no longer rises over the ranch each day, but it rises. When I look out my window, I make sure to say to that new day, "Glad you made it. Count me in the adventure." And off we go.

CHAPTER 35

SUNSETS

I've come to love much about Tucson. I'm back to living on a bigger chunk of land. Not 200,000 acres, but eight acres, enough that my neighbors and I can't yell across the fence to each other. I have season tickets to the University of Arizona's basketball games. Every February, the Old Pueblo, as the town is affectionately called, hosts Rodeo Days, a four-day stretch of barrel racing, roping, and bronc and bull riding. Trails for hikers and bikers crisscross through washes and over hills. Golf courses are found on every corner. Then there are the mountains. And margaritas. And mountains of margaritas.

But probably my all-time favorite event is something that happens every day of every year. Not mentioned in many travel guides, it comes free of cost. It started long before I was born and hopefully will continue long after my demise.

The sunset. That's what I'm talking about. In Tucson, the sun shines an average of three hundred fifty days per year, which means I get to watch the fiery ball sink out of sight in the West almost every day. In fall and winter, when the air is quick to usher out smog and haze, the sun's departure can be spectacular.

I've witnessed sunsets in Key West, Florida and Del Mar, California. I've seen the sun float above the edge of the South Dakota prairie, buoyed by summer's humidity. I cried leaning against the railing of a cruise ship as it entered a volcano crater in the Greek islands, the sun's last rays bouncing off perfectly calm water and "Chariots of Fire" echoing off the jutting mountains. I've seen the brilliance of a Santa Fe, New Mexico sunset with the purples, pinks, and peaches that inspired painters like Georgia O'Keefe.

Still, one of my favorite places to watch a sunset is in Tucson, especially on the golf course about four miles from my house. If I'm out at the range in late afternoon and hitting the ball well, I'll take a cart out and play nine holes. On almost every hole, I have a clear view of the western and eastern skies. The course is almost always deserted about then.

Somewhere around the eighth hole, the shadows begin to lengthen. I tee off facing west. I have to judge by the feel of the club head hitting the ball whether or not I'm in the fairway because glaring sunlight blinds me. About the time the ball drops into the tin cup, the show begins. A roadrunner dashes into the middle of the fairway and stops. Quail chortle. A coyote calls.

Then the sun throws its rays against the Santa Catalina Mountain's granite and gneiss, turning them a deep pink. For a few still moments, the world feels enormous. Nothing seems as important as being right there, right then. It's as if Mother Nature is calling out for everyone to stop what they're doing and pay attention to what's happening around them. The tops of the mountains hold their rosy hue as their base darkens. Quail bobble into their nests. A lone hawk swoops overhead. I hop in my cart and drive to the ninth tee, the western sky on fire with pink and orange clouds.

I've seen hundreds of these desert sunsets, some from the golf course, others from my backyard or through the windows of my car while driving. Occasionally, I pull over to watch the performance. Sunsets are like snowflakes and fingerprints—no two look exactly alike, but all leave their imprint on you and carry you through to the next day. All they require of you is to enjoy. Whether you do that with a smile or a tear or both is up to you.

ABOUT THE AUTHORS

H. Alan Day was part of the generation to grow up on the 200,000-acre Lazy B cattle ranch that straddled the high deserts of southern Arizona and New Mexico. The ranching and cowboying life appealed to him so much that after graduating from the University of Arizona, he returned to manage the Lazy B for the next 40 years. During his career, he received numerous awards for his dedicated stewardship of the land.

In the 1980s, Alan purchased a cattle ranch in Nebraska, followed by a ranch in South Dakota that he named Mustang Meadow Ranch. It became the first government-sponsored sanctuary for unadoptable wild horses. He was the first rancher to develop and successfully use a herd modification training program for cattle and wild mustangs. He tells his story of working with the mustangs in his award-winning memoir *The Horse Lover: A Cowboy's Quest to Save the Wild Mustangs.*

Alan also co-authored with his sister, Sandra Day O'Connor, the New York Times best-selling memoir *Lazy B*, which tells the story of the Day family and of growing up on the harsh yet beautiful ranch. Alan now divides his time between Tucson and Pinetop, Arizona.

Lynn Wiese Sneyd is a professional writer and owner of LWS Literary Services, an agency specializing in book publicity, query letters, book proposals, ghostwriting, and editing. In addition to co-authoring *The Horse Lover* and *Cowboy Up!,* Lynn wrote *Holistic Parenting* and co-authored the award-winning book *Healthy Solutions.* Her articles, essays, and poetry have appeared in various publications around the country. Visit her at www.lwsliteraryservices.com.

For a video tour of Lazy B, visit www.alandayauthor.com or text the word COWBOY to 66866.

Morgan James
Speakers Group

We connect Morgan James published authors with live and online events and audiences whom will benefit from their expertise.

Printed in the USA
CPSIA information can be obtained
at www.ICGtesting.com
JSHW022326140824
68134JS00019B/1320